Explorir
ITA

OTHER BOOKS IN THE *EXPLORING RURAL* SERIES

Series Editor: Andrew Sanger

Exploring Rural France
Andrew Sanger
Exploring Rural Spain
Jan S. McGirk

Forthcoming:

Exploring Rural Ireland
Exploring Rural Britain
Exploring Rural Portugal
Exploring Rural Austria
Exploring Rural Greece
Exploring Rural Germany

Exploring Rural
ITALY

MICHAEL LEECH

CHRISTOPHER HELM
London

© 1988 Michael Leech
Maps by Dave Henderson
Line illustrations by Lorna Turpin
Christopher Helm (Publishers) Ltd, Imperial House,
21-25 North Street, Bromley, Kent BR1 1SD

British Library Cataloguing in Publication Data

Leech, Michael
    Exploring rural Italy.
    1. Italy—Description and travel—1975 — Guide-
      books
    I. Title
    914.5'04928   DG430.2

ISBN 0-7470-2003-5

Typeset by Leaper and Gard, Bristol
Printed in Great Britain by
Billings and Sons Ltd, Worcester

CONTENTS

To my dear Mother,
Edith Hilda Leech (1909-1986)
who would have loved Italy

Italy — the regions and the routes

1 INTRODUCTION

Italy (It-a-ly) a republic, 116,225 square miles in area, a country of Southern Europe projecting into the Mediterranean Sea. Capital Rome.

Thus baldly does a dictionary define one of the fairest countries in the world, home of poets and painters, of ancient civilisations and of a nature so diverse and fascinating that its scenic pleasures never pall. Despite a long history of occupation by man (the Etruscans were in all probability first to bring civilisation, supplanting Paleolithic cave dwellers and the Neolithic tribes that followed them, and pre-dating the Roman Empire by several centuries), Italy has been one nation for only a short time — just over a hundred years. The bringing together of the north and the south, and the cementing of the whole peninsula with the take-over of the central Papal States, resulted in a modern nation that is united yet remarkably diverse. The city states, originally the idea of the mysterious Etruscans who built their towns on the high hills of Tuscany (Italian: Toscana) and farther inland at Orvieto, Volterra, Perugia and Arezzo, are still evident today, for many cities bear the stamp of a feudal family and places like Ferrara and Urbino are replete with mementoes of their medieval and Renaissance overlords. Fortunately, Italians for the most part are proud of their past, and architecture is carefully preserved even if it does represent an impediment to modern development.

The Italian genius for creating buildings of superlative beauty is reflected, oddly enough, in the remarkable and very complete system of autostrade, or toll-roads. The spectacular engineering of these roads as they pass through the often difficult terrain of the country, along with the elegance of bridges and support arches, is notable. Unfortunately, the system is so complete that it serves almost every town of any size, and consequently overrides lesser roads, making a book such as this difficult — very often cities are surrounded with such a ganglia of modern roads that the only reason for using them seems to be to get as swiftly as you can from one metropolis to another. I have suggested their use occasionally, for although expensive the autostrade can get you easily, if noisily and rather hair-raisingly, to exit points along the old country roads. They have also relieved old main roads of heavy traffic, making driving less hazardous and allowing more of a chance to see the scenery rather than just the back of the vehicle in front.

1

Although the cities of Italy are justly famed, and Rome (Roma), Florence (Firenze) and Venice (Venezia) feature on everybody's first-time itinerary, they are merely outlined here for they need a detailed exploration, usually on foot. You can choose them to stay in, but it is best not to use your car (indeed legislation will make it increasingly hard for anyone to drive into some cities) and parking is always a great problem. The idea of this book has been to suggest small cities and towns of particular interest as places to stop, with a route usually going out in a roughly circular path from them. For those not using a car there are usually good bus services, and many Italian towns are connected with a rail service. Cycling is not recommended except in areas such as the Emilia-Romagna where the land is undulating — Italy's mountains are steep and roads often precipitous, narrow and hard to navigate. Hiking is unusual in Italy, but there are some parts that lend themselves to good walks, but beware the intense sun, especially in the south. Since Italy's attractions are so numerous and so tightly packed in some places, things to see have sometimes been only briefly mentioned, and often a village that may have only minimal interest to the art lover will appear to have a ravishment of riches for those who seek atmosphere and scenery — the same goes for the open country so wherever possible subsidiary routes have been suggested, and aspects to suit as wide a variety of tastes.

Italy is a long country, boned down the centre with a spine of mountains, the Apennines (Appennino). They provide a barrier to crossing from east to west, but also magnificent scenery and wild deserted areas, as well as snow-capped ranges for ski enthusiasts. The north spreads down from the southern slopes of the Alps towards the extended valley of the Po, from its early springs near Turin, across the Lombardy plain finally to debouch just south of Venice. The Italian Lakes are spectacularly beautiful; the hills around Venice, often unvisited, rise above a coast that extends around towards Yugoslavia and the city of Trieste. The Riviera is justly famous, but even here you can get away from crowds and rapidly find yourself on tiny roads leading to spectacular hill-towns. Tuscany is well known to the visitor, but Umbria is much less visited and it is replete with ancient cities and deep green countryside. The shore of the Adriatic is flat, yet the buttresses of mountains rise beyond the sandy beaches of the Marches and the Abruzzo. The Roman countryside is special and south you come to Naples and its idyllic bay with superb little resorts; yet again a diversion can take you away from crowded places. Apulia is a hot land, still little discovered and yet filled with interest and with a coastline of extraordinary beauty. Calabria takes you through stretches of near empty countryside, strikingly wild, to Sicily (Sicilia) and a mysterious island famous for Greek ruins and a separate way of life. Sardinia (Sardegna), Italy's other major island, is mountainous and filled with character. Folk art is everywhere and festivals are common — is it wise to go to a tourist office either before you leave or as soon as you get to your principal destination to ask about current local attractions. There's a much quoted saying about Naples, supposedly summing up the beauty of that spot — 'see Naples and die'. I would say myself, 'see Italy and love, living for a lifetime of returns'.

Roads and Maps

As already stated Italy is very well served with major roads. The autostrade are marked on maps in strongly defined double lines and marked with the letter A. They are usually coloured red and yellow and exit points are marked. The old main roads are generally in a heavy red and marked with an N, sometimes with the addition of the word 'bis' or 'ter' to denote extensions or parallel routes. Secondary roads are in yellow, and are either wide for the principal ones or narrow for the next category, while the lowest category are marked in very narrow lines and are usually in grey or white. Distances between points are usually indicated in red with a kilometre distance. Maps do vary quite a bit, however, and each region seems to publish its own variety so the scale may vary. Get the biggest scale you can find; also check to see if there is a set of subsidiary maps (usually on the reverse) showing cultural, architectural, historical, gastronomic and folk attractions with a set of symbols.

Inevitably the selection of a series of routes is arbitrary and very much to the taste of the individual plotting the kind of trip he or she would prefer. You can follow the maps exactly, but it is always a good thing to allow for serendipity, that quality of surprise when a sudden challenge presents itself and you allow yourself to be beguiled into an adventure. It may be a sign saying a castle is open, a beckoning restaurant from a guide-book, a mere feeling that a certain turning has something interesting to show just around the corner, or a desire to look closer at a passing settlement. I hope these routes allow you to follow such urges, for Italy is filled with surprises and an unplanned turn into a road that is not on the route may provide an experience you never expected and *that* is the sort of thing that can make a holiday magic. Directions are usually quite good in Italy, with the autostrade being marked with green arrows with the city that is either closest or largest named as a destination point. The numbers of most major roads are usually to be found posted along the roadside. Historic sites or towns with particularly appealing aspects are usually posted with indications. Petrol stations are usually fairly frequent and will have (in the larger chains) shops and toilets. Roads are in general well maintained but they may be narrow — especially some of the suggested off-the-track ones in this book, so be prepared to have to stop frequently, or to manoeuvre past obstacles. In general, it will be found that there is not time to do a detailed visit to all the places mentioned in the time suggested — but this is merely included as a guide for those who don't necessarily want to do more than look from the car and perhaps stop three or four times. On some routes every town mentioned could take a half day's, even a day's exploration, so the choice as to what you do is very much up to you — usually a fast road is not too far away, if you have used up most of the day in exploration and can't hope to finish the route in the suggested time. It's a good idea to have a map book, such as those published by the main motoring organisations, in the car. T.C.I. (Touring Club Italiano) publishes maps and guides, available from McCarta Ltd in London.

Eating

Some of the finest food in the world is found in Italy, and even though the land is not good for agricultural development in many parts of the country, the areas that are suited are intensively farmed. Italy provides many delicacies that are unique, from the ham of Parma to the mushrooms of the northern woods, from wild game to a large variety of cheeses, from the ever-famous pasta in a vast range of styles and shapes to spiced meats and unusual preserves. Olives grow almost everywhere and the fruit and the oil are universally used. Rice is grown in the delta of the Po, providing the base for delicious risottos and puddings. All sorts of beans are used in dishes so that the vegetarian traveller can usually find menus in this admittedly meat-eating land. Bread is baked in a number of ways, the methods of preparing veal are many, and beef is prime, especially the famous *bue* of Tuscany. Fish is less plentiful than once it was, yet the many little ports around the coast (and a glance will show you that there is a great deal of coastline in Italy!) still offer fresh fish which is always available at some local restaurant — prepared simply, swiftly and with a genuine care to provide the customer with an increasingly rare experience, the taste of fresh seafood. Don't for a moment imagine that the national dish is only pasta and its ubiquitous tomato sauce as found in too many restaurants beyond the borders of Italy. Marco Polo, may, by tradition, have imported noodles from the Orient, but the Italian ingenuity has transformed the basic elements into dishes of amazing variety. Pasta, by the way, is often presented as a starter to a meal, with lightly grilled meats or fish to follow. Almost every town will have a special dish to offer, from the garlic and basil pesto with pine-nuts of Genoa to polenta as served in Bergamo.

Wines are another area where you have a vast and amazing choice and vines are grown almost all over the country, so there are many different kinds, from the classic chiantis of Tuscany to robust and heavy reds in the south. Nor is the range limited to red and white: the Italians make a fine rosé, a superb dessert wine (vini santi — from dried grapes) and even a champagne-style wine which is very good and very cheap, though tending to be sweeter than French originals. Local people will be pleased if you ask for the wine of the region and even more so if you find it commendable. Visits to vineyards in the main areas are possible and if it is likely that you want to plan visits, then ask ahead of time as to where there are such places. I've included some in this book, but it is also sensible to look out for signs as you progress through vine-growing areas. The only time when you won't be so welcome is in the autumn (usually late September through October) when the grapes are being gathered in and crushed, and everyone is needed for the work.

Most restaurants will take credit cards, and you will find bargains in some of the smaller towns, where a full meal can still seem very reasonable when you consider the quality of the food — and the wine of course is not expensive. The only thing with Italian meals is to allow lots of time to eat them — a lunch, or a dinner, is not something to be rushed through, so if you want a quick eat-and-run meal then you would be wiser to use a snack bar or a small café and eat fairly straightforwardly. Or else you can pack a picnic — a very good idea for there are many locations just asking for you to stop and have a meal in the sunshine *al fresco*. Italy also abounds in the kind of food shops that stock marvellous picnic foods — salamis, ham, salad, cheese, crusty loaves of bread, delicious butter, marvellous ripe fruit and, of course, all kinds of beer, wine and fruit drinks. So be prepared and pack a picnic basket in the car for such delicious holiday fare! A good restaurant guide book: *La Guida d'Italia* (annual paperback).

Accommodation

There are plenty of places to stay in Italy — the country is well equipped with accommodation in a wide range of prices from luxurious hotels (and no hotels come in a more luxurious range than in Italy: their best hotels are the best in the world with spectacular sites and service that makes even the Swiss palace-hotels look ordinary) to simple and cheap *pensione*. Most are in the centre of cities, of course, but even villages will have well-managed places often combining rustic charm with plain yet quite adequate accommodation. They are usually indicated with signs, or a visit to the local garage or café will usually provide you with ideas of what's available. Even quite small and unprepossessing towns will have a good small hostelry of moderate price, usually with a light breakfast added on as an extra. Tourist information offices will provide free lists of hotels, and the many small local tourist boards carry out the same function for their immediate areas. *The Travellers' Handbook*, obtainable from the Italian State Tourist Offices is a handy publication for the addresses of tourist offices as well as other basic information.

Italy has about 40,000 hotels, many clustered in the resort areas and cities, and classified into five 'star' categories. The top category are the expensive ones and in addition carry an extra VAT tax over and above the standard rate applicable. The cost of a room is not much more for two occupants than for one, especially in double-bedded rooms, and nowadays most rooms will have a private bathroom. You can make reservations ahead through the offices maintained by hotel chains, but most of these are top category. If you want to rent a villa or a chalet, then check the local tourist board. There also exists an exchange system for people wishing to let Italians stay in their homes in exchange for a base in Italy. Motels are very popular in Italy and can be found on many main roads and autostrade — usually modern and functional, they can be singularly charmless but are useful if your time for looking around is limited. The Club Alpino Italiano has mountain huts or *rifugi Alpini* for those who are looking for very simple places to stay in the high districts.

In addition, there are hostels for YHA members and students' hostels and firms exist to rent cottages and farmhouses on a self-catering basis. For those looking for campsites (which are popular and cheap) there are more than 1,600 approved sites in Italy with a detailed list published by the Touring Club Italiano. Accommodation is usually not hard to find, although the holiday months of July and August are usually well booked. For those looking for very unusual places to stay, such as palaces and abbeys, the tourist office can help with a list of such places, but again they are often expensive. Hotels will usually offer credit card facilities and the bigger ones will exchange money but it's always wisest to do that at a bank.

Driving in Italy

This book is principally for the driver who is either taking a car or hiring one when there. For British drivers, there are some points to remember — you must have a working left-hand mirror (driving is, of course, on the right) and, while you do not need an international driver's licence, it is as well to carry an Italian translation of your British one. Distances are all in kilometres — and petrol in litres. Note that distances in this book are very rough indications since many of the routes are expandable and the total distance given is intended as a guide to the amount of driving you will need to do. Ten kilometres down or up a mountain road can take quite a time too, remember! Italian drivers can be impatient and sound their horns: don't let yourself be upset and keep a cool head when striking a bottleneck — as you may well do in some of the areas such as the Lakes where routes can be very narrow with high banks. Take especial care at roundabouts (traffic circles). Road signs are now almost totally universal, so the ones you meet with in Italy should be quite familiar. The autostrade system is marvellous and is well marked, bearing a fee for the distance covered which you pay when you make your exit. At times I have suggested using the autostrade as a way of getting swiftly to an area, or else returning fast to your base when other roads offer little in terms of interest. Certainly if you are driving all the way to your destination* they are immensely helpful if you want to get to Tuscany, or the Abruzzo, or Calabria quickly and smoothly. In some places the motorways actually iron out the landscape, and in Italy there are some formidable barriers to communication.

For those taking bus or train connections and then exploring, there are detailed maps, although except in the towns (where it is often almost mandatory) walking is not something the Italians do much of. Note that Rome is now closed to much private traffic and if you stay there, or visit, you will probably have to leave your car outside and take public transport

---

*Note. For those wishing to take a holiday and not wanting to drive all the way through France, there are package holidays through several organisations that will include a self-drive car — Alitalia, the national airline with offices in main cities, can help with suggestions and flight times.

to your destination. Be sure to lock your car securely and remove or conceal any valuables.

And Finally ...

It is a most beautiful country, with marvellous things to see and do. A little Italian will help a great deal (the Italians will love it if you try a few words) and it is wise to take a dictionary and a phrase book, although in this country of flamboyant gestures you can communicate a lot with your hands and your body! On the routes remember that the places and roads are only suggestions, leading to places that happen to be personal favourites or have come well recommended to me. Serendipity, as I've said, should always play a large part in any visit to this green-and-golden land and if something appeals that I haven't noted, then let your heart rule your head and enjoy what is offered. Italy is filled with surprises and in many years of visiting this ancient and hospitable land I have always had the best of holidays and can quite truthfully say that never once have I ever been bored.

Metric Conversion Tables

All measurements are given in metric units. For readers more familiar with the imperial system, the accompanying tables are designed to facilitate quick conversion to imperial units. Bold figures in the central columns can be read as either metric or imperial: e.g. 1kg = 2.20lb or 1lb = 0.45kg.

mm		in	cm		in	m		yds
25.4	1	.039	2.54	1	0.39	0.91	1	1.09
50.8	2	.079	5.08	2	0.79	1.83	2	2.19
76.2	3	.118	7.62	3	1.18	2.74	3	3.28
101.6	4	.157	10.16	4	1.57	3.66	4	4.37
127.0	5	.197	12.70	5	1.97	4.57	5	5.47
152.4	6	.236	15.24	6	2.36	5.49	6	6.56
177.8	7	.276	17.78	7	2.76	6.40	7	7.66
203.2	8	.315	20.32	8	3.15	7.32	8	8.75
228.6	9	.354	22.86	9	3.54	8.23	9	9.84

g		oz	kg		lb	km		miles
28.35	1	.04	0.45	1	2.20	1.61	1	0.62
56.70	2	.07	0.91	2	4.41	3.22	2	1.24
85.05	3	.11	1.36	3	6.61	4.83	3	1.86
113.40	4	.14	1.81	4	8.82	6.44	4	2.48
141.75	5	.18	2.27	5	11.02	8.05	5	3.11
170.10	6	.21	2.72	6	13.23	9.65	6	3.73
198.45	7	.25	3.18	7	15.43	11.26	7	4.35
226.80	8	.28	3.63	8	17.64	12.87	8	4.97
255.15	9	.32	4.08	9	19.84	14.48	9	5.59

ha		acres
0.40	1	2.47
0.81	2	4.94
1.21	3	7.41
1.62	4	9.88
2.02	5	12.36
2.43	6	14.83
2.83	7	17.30
3.24	8	19.77
3.64	9	22.24

Metric to imperial conversion formulae

	multiply by
cm to inches	0.3937
m to feet	3.281
m to yards	1.094
km to miles	0.6214
km^2 to square miles	0.3861
ha to acres	2.471
g to ounces	0.03527
kg to pounds	2.205

2 PIEDMONT AND THE LAKES
(Piemonte and Lombardia)

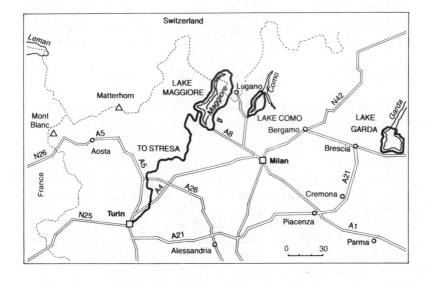

In Moncalieri, a town not far from Turin, there was a widow called Madonna Zilia Duca ... it is a general custom of all the women of the town to kiss all the strangers who come to their homes or by whom they are visited, and to entertain everyone in a familiar way; but she shunned all these practices and lived to herself.

Opening lines of a novella by Matteo Bandello

The town of Moncalieri is now almost an extension of Turin's southerly suburbs, although it retains its castle, once the favoured residence of Victor Emmanuel II. It's doubtful that the women folk of the town would be quite so forthcoming as they were in Bandello's 16th century (he was a monk who wrote licentious short stories) yet you will find as you explore mountainous Piedmont that the old cliché 'the natives are friendly' still seems true, although they are initially reserved. Piedmont is known as a cradle of the nation and the name is descriptive of the region — at the foot of the mountains. Here the second of Italy's wars against the Austrian occupying forces found strong support from Cavour in 1859,

Medieval castle, Turin

and Piedmont's king (Victor Emmanuel II) found his patrimony growing to include much of northern Italy, eventually merging into the new nation.

The region now occupies the Po valley and a ring of encircling mountains, while to the east a long and roughly triangular plain abuts Lombardy. In the north-eastern corner the border is composed of the long arm of Lake Maggiore while Lake Orta is within the region, shadowed by the hills rising to the heights of the Alps. Lombardy holds the other lakes of the famous district, stretching to the Veneto and Garda. Here is to be found some of the most sublime scenery in Italy, and a lambent climate that makes gardens grow extravagantly, spilling foliage over old walls and terraces. Small wonder visitors have always been attracted to the area which Italy shares in part with the neighbouring Swiss canton of Ticino. One of the great attractions of the lakes is its magnificent gardens — you could drive around and do nothing but visit them, but there is much else to do and some marvellous places to stay. It should be noted that public transport is good, so if you decide to leave your car and take bus or train and boat, then the relief will be pleasurable, for in the summer season roads can get fearfully overcrowded. Best time to go is spring or autumn, when painters and photographers will find a plethora of memorable subjects.

One-time capital of a kingdom until a century and a quarter ago, the city of **TURIN** (Italian: Torino) (pop: 1,250,000) is a relatively unvisited city. This is a pity, despite the city's undeniably extensive industrial base — it is the home of Fiat — for it is well located in its flat river valleys, rimmed with mountain peaks. The city has fine galleries and archaeological museums, and is laid out with 18th-century precision upon Roman foundations. Its character is Baroque and grandiose, soberly elegant, planned in neat straight lines. The effect is harmonious and attractive; the cleaning of 18th- and 19th-century buildings continues and the many walking streets and the arcades make Turin something of a model. The gastronomy of Turin is very much for those with a sweet tooth; the pastries and chocolate are universal. In addition, it is the home of Italian vermouths and there are good wines to go with such marvellous specialities as dishes with truffles.

If you choose to make the city a stopover point then consider visits to the following places of interest: the central Piazza S. Carlo, an example of good planning in a direct line between the railway station and the royal palace on the Piazza Castello; the multi-styled Palazzo Madama; the Palazzo Reale (once residence of the Kings of Sardinia); the Roman Porta Palatina; the Piazza San Giovanni and the Duòmo which is Renaissance (commenced in 1491) with a slightly earlier campanile; it is the home of the Chapel of the Holy Shroud, lined in black marble — the shroud itself is rarely on show. Near the cathedral are the ruins of a Roman theatre. All the buildings and museums are within easy walking distance of each other; the Museum of Antiquities in the Palazzo dell'Accademia delle Scienze contains the Museum of Antiquities and the Egyptian collection, which is particularly extensive and benefited in the first place from Napoleon's campaigns to Egypt. On the second floor is the Sabauda Gallery, strong in Dutch and Flemish paintings. The Museum of Ancient Art is housed in the Palazzo Madama. One of the pleasures of Turin is walking, and there is an opera house and theatres. Hotels are mostly near the station and a well-recommended restaurant, expensive but very atmospheric, is the one in the **Villa Sassi** at Strada Traforo del Pino 47 (011-890 556), closed Sundays and August.

To the Lakes at Stresa

1 day or longer/180km approx/from Turin to Stresa

This route is a direct one, going from Turin to Stresa on Lake Maggiore, which is used as a centre for the next route.

Leave Turin on the road running north-east towards Settimo, by-passing it along the down-flowing River Po to arrive at **CHIVASSO**, a distance of approximately 30km. Here it is worth a stop to look at the fine 15th-century church and its unusual doorway; within there is a polychrome Pieta. Continue along the N11 until, just past the entrance to the N26 (direction: Ivrea), you will find a road running across the plain towards Mazze, a small town on a crossroads. Continue on along the valley of the Baltea until you rejoin the N26 at Strambino — here you will begin to see the mountains clearly and especially to the north-east the stark mass of the Serra d'Ivrea, a moraine wall formed by glacier actions. (If you decided on the more direct N26 you will have passed the Lake of Candia *en route* to this point.) Continue north to **IVREA**, a town in a picturesque location where a king of Italy was crowned in 1002. There is plenty to see in this small settlement, home of Olivetti for almost 80 years,

and there is a carnival in February. It was once a Roman stronghold against hill tribes, and Roman fragments can be seen in various buildings, notably the Bishop's Palace and the Civic Museum. Two bridges cross the river, one from the early 18th century. There is a three-towered castle (one tower, making up the total to four, has been ruined) dating from the 14th century, and a fine belltower of 1041 in the public gardens. The church has vanished, but the cathedral dates in part from the same era.

Continue out of the town along a road (steep and winding) towards Biella over the Serra, descending into the valley of the Elvo to cross the little national park of La Bessa, passing a new road as it enters Mongrande. (This road, when complete, will connect with the N26 up the valley.) A route from Ivrea takes you up to **BORGOFRANCO** where there are thermal waters, and also allows access by a narrow mountain road to Biella. A short journey of a dozen km up to the N26 brings you to **PONT ST MARTIN**, a small town on the border of Val d'Aosta, with castle ruins and a Roman bridge from the 1st century BC, standing amidst vineyards and, as its name suggests, close to a French-speaking corner of Italy.

On the approach to Biella an interesting detour may be made to the left up towards the Sanctuary of Oropa, via Pollone. Here you can find the **Parco Burcina** and a vast array of rhododendrons to the right of the little road which joins the route to **OROPA**, a popular place of pilgrimage in the mountains at over 1000m, where St Eusebius of Vercelli supposedly hid a sacred image. Onwards are ski-stations connected by cable car (two routes) up Mt Mucrone to enjoy fine views.

BIELLA (pop: 54,000) is built on two levels, and there is a cable-railway joining them. There are fine churches on the Biella Piano (lower level), and at Biella Piazzo (upper level) good views and several elegant Renaissance palaces. The main industry of Biella is textiles, particularly wool, but it makes a good centre for local exploration. Nearby are **GAGLIANICO** with a striking 16th-century castle **GRAGLIA** — with its sanctuary and **CANDELO** along a rural road on the valley of the Cervo, where there is an unusual fortress and foodstore, built in the 14th century. Continue from Biella towards Borgosesia, then turn sharp right towards Cassato, and on down to **ROVASENDA** where there is a castle on the banks of the river of the same name. Then turn left to Gattinara and across the Sesia to **ROMAGNANO**, where there are papermaking

and cotton spinning mills. [A road south will take you to **VERCELLI** —
well worth a detour all along the Sesia valley among its rice fields. The
home of Il Sodoma and a whole school of 16th-century painters. The
church has connections with an English king, Henry III, and is a striking
13th-century array of towers and arcades — Sant' Andrea. There is a fine
duòmo and also a museum of paintings, the Borgogna. Piazza Cavour
with its arcades and belltower will appeal to photographers. There is a
well-recommended restaurant called **Il Paiolo** on the via Garibaldi
(0161-53577) serving (not surprisingly) good risottos.]

From Romagnano Sesia continue on a back road, rather than the main
road towards Lake Orta, passing through **BOCA** with its church, or make
a detour up as far as **VARALLO**, a town of charm which makes a good
centre for mountain walks or excursions to **SACRO MONTE**, with its
many chapels and statues. From just south of Varallo a road cuts across
the mountains to Lake Orta, which from the principal route we join near
Gozzano on the main road. Turn left and continue along the west bank of
the lake at a junction near which stands a watch tower, the ancient
Buccione. This restored Lombard tower stands on a hill, and marks the
end of Lake Orta. Follow signs for Omegna, along the west side of the
lake for views across the narrow stretch of water towards Orta. From
PELLA boats can be taken across the lake, but this route continues on to
OMEGNA, a resort with a medieval bridge and some interesting houses.
From here you can drive directly over the mountain at a spot just south of
the town, taking the sign for Armeno and then Stresa. However, it would
be a pity not to go on to **ORTA** either along the coast or down from the
crossroads at Armeno. This small town on a peninsula is extremely pretty
and has fine views to the Island of San Giulio (boats ply from the square)
where you can walk along the sole street admiring the houses with their
balconies and gardens. Be sure to visit the Basilica with its black marble
pulpit, oddly carved and supported with columns. Back in Orta walk up
the Sacro Monte by a path to the top, offering good views from the
terraces of one of the many chapels. The restaurant of the **Hotel San
Rocco** at Via Gippini 11 (0322-90222), is locally renowned — especially
the sweet dishes.

Return the way you came towards Stresa, with an alternative hill road
if wished directly on from Armeno (instead of turning right) towards
Monte Mottarone. This is a road of many curves, but the view from here
is wonderful, over the lakes to the mountains and south across the
countryside beyond Lake Maggiore. Heading down the Stresa road you
pass alpine gardens (open all summer until the end of October, fine views)
and down through **GIGNESE** where there is a museum of umbrellas and
sunshades, to **VEZZO** with its golf course, and so along more twisting
turns down to the lakeside and **STRESA** itself (see next route).

Around Lake Maggiore

1 day/215km/from Stresa (NOTE: take passports since part of the route includes Switzerland)

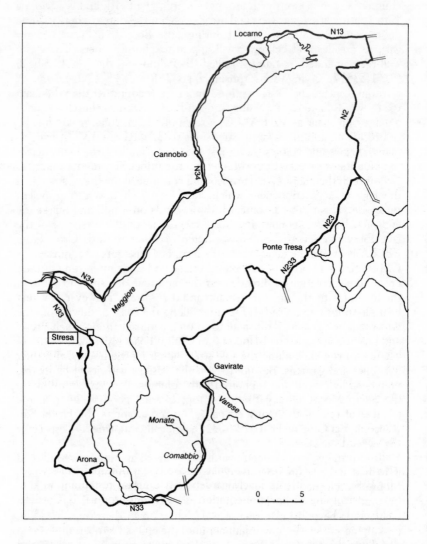

Using Stresa as a base, the route will take you around the shores of Lake Maggiore yet also into the hinterland to allow distant views and impressions of the lake scenery. First, however, you may want to explore **STRESA** itself, and the neighbouring islets of the lake — but these will need additional time, and you should set aside a day to go by boat to the three main islands, which can easily be seen from Stresa — Isola Madre, Isola Pescatori and, most incredible, Isola Bella. They are known as the

Isola Bella, Lake Maggiore

Borromean Islands from the family which still controls much of Lake Maggiore. Isola Madre is farthest from Stresa and is a botanical garden noted for its fine shrubs which grow in profusion; Isola Pescatori is a fishing village and Isola Bella is a series of tiers of formal gardens, looking rather like a floating teatray replete with balustrades and spirelets. Stresa is a marvellous centre for exploring all the lakes — although this chapter uses it for but one route, a small town with fine views across the lake. Of recent years it has become popular as a conference venue with such luxurious hotels as CIGA's **Hotel des Iles Borromées** on the lakefront (with good, but expensive, restaurant; 0323-30431) and the **Hotel Villa Aminta** (also restaurant; 0323-30505) being busy with international delegates. There are several fine villas in the town; note particularly the Villa Pallavicino with its lovely garden. An unusual restaurant in the town, specialising in the presentation of wild mushrooms, is **Cardini** (0323-30370).

Leave Stresa by the little road going up the hill to Someraro, but turn left before this village to pass through the upper stretches of the town towards Vedasco. Here, follow the road to Carpugnino and so on up the valley with the lake hidden by the mound of Motta Rossa until you arrive at **MASSINO VISCONTI** with its castle above the Torrente Erno. Continue towards Invorio and then turn left in the centre of the village for Paruzzaro on the edge of a *parco naturale* above the end of the lake. To the left on the lakeshore is **ARONA** (pop: 17,500) which is a town with some fine buildings and also serves as the terminus of the lake steamer services. Just north of the town is a curiosity — a gigantic statue of a saint (Carlo Borromeo) dating from the 17th century, which can be ascended for the view, and is known as the San Carlone. The upper road continues along the park border then turns to join N32 and almost immediately N33 towards **SESTO CALENDE**, also situated in a natural park abutting the lower east side of the lake, a town with a name of Roman origin and a good Romanesque church containing frescoes. Continue on N33 for about 1km until a signed small road takes you towards Oneda to the left and on along the south shore of the Lake of Comabbio. Crossing the narrow neck of land between the Lakes of Comabbio and Varese brings you eventually to the small town of **GAVIRATE** on the north shore of the latter lake.

[If you wish to make an excursion you can stop here and take a lake boat to the tiny isle of Virginia where there is a museum of objects from early lake settlements. From here you can strike down along the lakeshore to the interesting old brick cloisters at **VOLTORRE** (and on, if you wish, towards Varese, following this little lakeside road most of the way). Unfortunately, the lake of Varese is now much polluted. **VARESE** (pop: 95,000) is a small compact town with a thriving footwear industry. It is situated at a point from which you can obtain good views, as far as the snow-topped Alps on a clear day. There is a public garden modelled after the palace of Schönbrunn's pleasure grounds in Vienna, and on its esplanade is the town museum, housed in the Villa Mirabello. The oldest building is the Baptistery (13th century) next to the basilica of San Vittore (large 17th-century pictures and ornate wood-carvings). It is usually possible to ascend the nearby campanile, a separate structure in an older style dating from the 17th century. The *sacro monte* near the town (about 8km to the north-west) can be visited either by car or a bus service. Above the village of Monte is Monte delle Tre Croci (views) and farther on, after you leave this small resort with its hotels, you come to Campo Dei Fiori which has spectacular views of the whole area.]

Continue from Gavirate along the valley on the N394 and when you come to Gemonio turn right along a small road towards Azzio and then on along the *Val Cuvia* to a junction where you turn right. This road will take you up between the hills until you reach **MESENZANA**, where there are ruins and where you may, if you wish, visit local stables to procure horses for a hill ride. Turn sharp right for N233 and drive towards Ponte Tresa. The village at the juncture is **GHIRLA**, standing by its tiny lake set like a jewel in the mountains and often crowded with skaters in the winter. If you care to backtrack along the lake you will come to a turning on the left for **MONTE PIAMBELLO**. It is very narrow and steep but will reward you with a spectacular view of the Lake of Lugano, almost all of which is in Swiss territory.

N233 stops at **PONTE TRESA**, the border village which is actually in two parts — the River Tresa marks the border, and you cross into Switzerland where the road becomes number 23 and skirts parts of the Lake of Lugano. A turning to the right will take you to the very smart resort town of **LUGANO** with its elegant lake promenade and stylish,

Lake Maggiore

expensive hotels. Otherwise, continue on the same road towards Locarno. Just before it crosses the motorway to join 2 going north you can enter the motorway if you wish and go fast up to the Plain of Magadino. You will have to leave it just before this point, however, at Monte Ceneri to continue on 2 until Cadenazzo. Here you will take a small road across the plain to the left, direction Gudo, crossing the River Ticino, which gives this canton of Switzerland (the only Italian-speaking one) its name. There are views down to the end of Lake Maggiore to the left. Turn left at the village of Progero towards **LOCARNO**, a pleasant town, less smart than Lugano but very agreeable. Pass through the town, unless you wish to stop and explore, and continue across the flat valley of the River Maggia and follow directions for Ascona, then towards the border with Italy at Loro. The road follows the lake closely; there are views across to the range of hills on the east side of the lake, the Gambarogna.

From the border, the road hugs the lakeside, hemmed in by the hills and with the far shore constantly in view across the water. It is likely to be calm, yet Maggiore does have a history of storms, so you may see the water suddenly lashed with rain and wind — a northerly wind blows until mid-morning, then a southerly, yet another can spring up from the Gulf of Pallanza. The first settlement along the road of any size is

CANNOBIO, with a pier for boats and many camping sites in the valley of the Cannabino. A side trip could carry you 3km up the valley to the **ORRIDO SANT'ANNA**. This is a wild and narrow pass down which tumbles a waterfall — a good site for a picnic. Cannobio itself has a handsome Renaissance cupola'd church. In spring this journey south is the most romantic — with the lake softly misted in the early morning and every house and garden wall smothered in new foliage and early blossom. Small wonder British visitors of the 18th and 19th centuries loved it! It must have seemed worlds away from the dankness of the north. The only problem now is the narrowness of these roads — the Italians seem to know to a millimetre how wide are their cars — the foreigner is not so aware, and I well recall seeing an English driver nearly reduced to tears by the well-meant comments of the local people as a large truck edged by his little sedan, almost but not quite pushing it to the edge of the road — a steep slope down to the blue water below. Be prepared for stops and starts and allow lots of time to drive from one town to another.

The next town of any size is **CANNERO RIVIERA**, in the shadow of Monte Carza; you can climb nearby Monte Zeda which is much higher. The romantic ruins on the twin islands in the lake are said to be those of the Cannero family, robber barons, but are likely to be more recent than the medieval castles of local lords. The dramatically placed church above the town is the Carmine. You can drive inland to Intra from here, over the hills and the high pass of Spalavera. Continue on past **GHIFFA**, prettily placed on a promontory, and arrive at **INTRA VERBANIA**, which has ferry connections across the lake to Laveno (regular frequent service, passengers and cars). A road from Intra takes you up the mountain a distance of about 10km to **PREMENO**, a high resort with a wonderful panorama. Intra is an industrial town, but it has spectacular gardens (mostly private) with one marvellous one — the **Villa Taranto**, a botanical garden open from April to October. There are many rare species of exotic plants and floral shows, as well as research laboratories. The gardens are beautifully laid out and maintained.

At this point the road rounds a spur of land and heads towards **PALLANZA**, a beautiful little town with rare plants in its gardens and fine magnolia trees along the lakeside, which has excellent views of the Borromean Islands. Its full name is Pallanza Verbania, the addition referring to the Latin name of the lake, in turn named after the verbena which is common here. In the town there are good shops and a market place, with churches that are perhaps more interesting from the outside but which add considerably to the charm of this typical town. Boats for hire and tennis courts on the lakefront.

The road continues to stay close to the lake as you leave Pallanza. Across the arm of the water beyond the islands there are views of Baveno; this is a lovely drive taking you around the end of the lake and picking up the lakeside again after you turn left in the direction of Stresa.

BAVENO is a quiet town with perfect views across to Pallanza and the islands. It is a resort in a beautiful situation, and is also a spa town with curative springs for diuretic problems. There is a pretty town square, and a church of considerable antiquity (restored in the 14th century) still containing an ancient baptistery of the 6th century as well as frescoes, and, to indicate that it was once bigger, there are arcades of a one-time cloister, now a side of the square. A curious house is the Casa Morandi with its outside staircases. From Baveno it is a very short distance back to Stresa along a road giving constant views of the lake and the islands, and with many villas all lined up behind gardens to share the famous views. There are good walks in the wooded countryside and in Stresa a little funicular ascends to Monte Mottarone. **MOTTARONE** itself is a short distance from the summit of the mountain which offers splendid views as far as the high Alps and, in the opposite direction, the sprawl of Milan.

Around Lake Como
½-1 day/90km (extensions possible)/from Bellagio

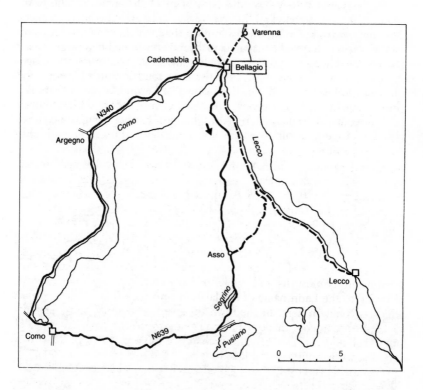

It would be practical, perhaps, to suggest Como as a base, but practicality is hardly a virtue on an Italian holiday! The dreamlike, gentle scenery of the lakes is best appreciated from one of the many small towns along their shores, and in this case the little settlement of Bellagio makes a perfect setting. You will need to cross Como on one of the car ferries and, if you are staying for a few days in Bellagio (and be warned, it is very tempting!), you may want to take another ferry across to Varenna and follow the lakeside road towards the mountains to explore the upper arm of Como, returning to cross back on the other side as far as Menaggio (passenger ferry) or, a little farther on, Cadenabbia (car ferry). Alternatively, there is a good route along the lakeside south to Lecco and beyond, returning on the far shore along this arm of the lake, known as the Lago di Lecco. (**LECCO** — pop: 60,000 — is a manufacturing centre and has an ancient bridge across the River Adda. It was the home of the novelist Alessandro Manzoni; his house is now a museum. There are rock-climbing and ski-centres in the vicinity in the mountains to the east.)

BELLAGIO is a small town situated right at the point of the inverted Y shape of Lake Como. It is a quiet resort with spectacular views and good hotels and lakeside cafés. Like Como there is silk-weaving here. There is an ancient church with sculptures and on the hill above the town the Villa Serbelloni with a beautiful park open in the summer. The town, with its stepped streets, is a fine centre for walks and one might be made to Villa Melzi 2km away — this Empire-style villa has fine gardens with statues and a doorway attributed to Bramante, brought from an earlier house. Lovely views over the lake to the west. Souvenirs of Bellagio include olive-wood carvings. Take the road south towards Civenna and ascend the hill beside Monte Garnasca. Just beyond Civenna there is a high point with a fantastic view over the Lago di Lecco and back towards Bellagio (chapel of the Madonna del Ghisallo). Farther along you come to **MAGREGLIO**, a village where you may make the ascent of Monte

Lake Como

Primo on foot and there are horse-riding facilities here. Continue on along the valley of the Lambro. The narrow and steep Valassina continues to Asso, where it is possible to connect with the route if you have chosen the shore road as far as **ONNO**, where there is a sailing school and a ferry station for boats to and from Lecco, thence up the Valbrano to Asso. On to **CANZO** where there are information services and horses for riding — this is a resort town. Continue on along the shores of the pretty little Lake of Segrino. Close to the larger Lake of Pusiano you join, to the right, the road to **ERBA**, a town in the agriculturally rich Brianza. There are villas, an open-air theatre and an archaeological museum. Drive on to Como through villages along the edge of the wide valley; you can skirt the city if you wish and continue along the west bank of the lake.

COMO (pop: 100,000) is a major centre of the silk industry, and you can wander around the warehouses and stalls looking at and buying, if you wish, lengths of the fine fabric. The city preserves a Roman street plan and the regular lines of the *castrum* are still evident. It is a major centre for tourism, handsomely sited at the southern end of its lake and shadowed by the bulk of Monte Brunate to the north-west. The Piazza Cavour is beside the lake and the landing stages for the many steamer services, and from it the Via Plinio goes to the handsome arcaded *Broletto*, once the *palazzo comunale*, with a 13th-century tower. The cathedral is Gothic, although not finished until the Renaissance, so you have a harmonious arrangement of Gothic architecture and later decoration. Within are fine tapestries and a rose window and elements from an earlier catherdral — the stone lions and a madonna — while the pretty little baptistery should not be overlooked. There are good pictures and some lively sculptures. Nearby is the Bishop's Palace and a handsome early 19th-century theatre with a classical portico. Near the 17th-century town hall is the early church of S. Fedele with its odd, five-sided apse with Eastern influences (fine interior) and the church of S. Cecilia has ancient columns in its porch from a Roman temple. Along the boulevards Cattaneo and Battisti there are remains of city fortifications as well as towers — at the Porta Nuova, the Porta Vittoria (12th century) and the Torre di S. Vitale. S. Abbondio is worth seeking out even in its unsalubrious setting of ugly modern buildings — it has two towers and the 11th-century building has a well-restored apse with frescoes. It was once the cathedral. The Museo Civico (closed Mon) has an extensive archaeological collection.

There are several good restaurants in Como — **Vecchie Cantine dei Jesumin**, noted as the best in town (book in the evening) not far from the old centre (031-266030) and, less expensive, **La Fiorentina** (031-271042) with a garden.

Take the lake road from the city north towards **CERNOBBIO** where poor Queen Caroline lived for a time in 1816 at the Villa d'Este, now a grand hotel with splendid lakefront position. From Cernobbio you can

21

walk up Monte Bisbino for views across to the far shore. The next town along the lake is **MOLTRASIO** where, in the Villa Salterio, Bellini composed *Norma*. Opposite and on the green east-facing shore is **TORNO**, a medieval settlement with two ancient churches, one with a pointed façade. (There are several ferry services across the lake, and a hydrofoil also plies up and down from Como to Colico at the far north end of the lake, but if you have time it is better to take the slower ferries for the views.) **TORRIGIO** is at the narrowest neck of the lake, and the road continues along the lakeshore, under green hills, past **NESSO** on the opposite bank, a pretty village with a waterfall called the *orrido di Nesso* and a short distance away the gardens of the Villa Trotti. On the route we come to the resort of **ARGEGNO**, at the end of the valley of the Intelvi (worth a detour). From here you start to see the higher mountains to the north. Up the valley is **LANZO D'INTELVI**, which is a good centre for mountain walks with eventual views over the neighbouring Lake Lugano. From here there is a cable car down to the Lake.

Next along the shore comes **SALA COMACINA** with its attendant islet with the ruins of a medieval fortress, as well as several churches — it is now a resort for artists. The town has a charming campanile. There is a good church tower also at **SPURANO**. On the way to Lenno look for the Villa Arcanti (gardens open once a week). At **LENNO**, S. Stefano is built on the site of Pliny's home; his lower villa was the Comedia — the other, the Tragedia, is at Bellagio. Look for the church of S. Andrea on the hillside in fine early Lombard style. The road now enters the Tremezzina Riviera, a beautiful garden-clad shore with **TREMEZZO** a delightful resort town with particularly good gardens, filled with azaleas and rare blooms, in terraces rising around the 18th-century Villa Carlotta; particularly good in spring. From here you can see Bellagio on its point, and reach it from the ferry at **CADENABBIA**, a charming resort in one of the prettiest locations.

If you wish to continue on the west shore, drive up as far as **DONGO** where Mussolini and his mistress were captured in 1945, but you will have to retrace your route or else drive right around the lake to get back to Varenna and the opposite shore for ferry connections to Bellagio.

Around Lake Garda

1 day or more/95km (or 195 if whole lake circumnavigated)/from Sirmione

The large lake to the east is Garda, a beautiful stretch of water and not as well known as the three to the west. It is the biggest, however, and offers spectacular scenery, particularly along the northern arm with high cliffs crowding upon the water. You could choose to stay at a large centre such as Verona in the Veneto, and have easy access to the lake, but perhaps a small centre such as Sirmione on its peninsula is more inviting. (The other main lake, Iseo, while smaller than the rest, also offers intriguing

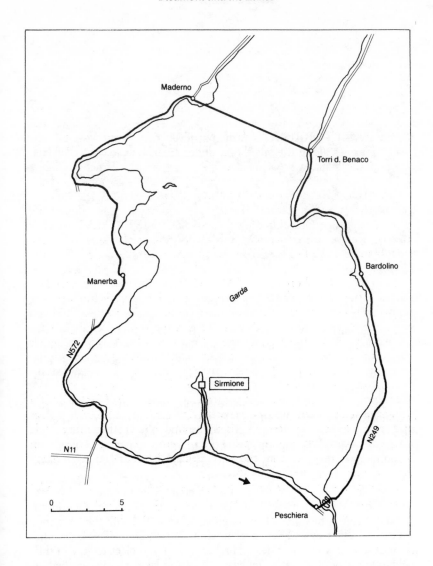

scenery but can be visited from your earlier base of Bellagio: equally so from Sirmione.)

SIRMIONE sits at the end of an unusual peninsula thrusting 5km north into the lake from its southern shore. It is a spa and resort, with many hotels on its rocky point. There is a modern spa establishment for taking the sulphurous waters, and it has been favoured since the Romans — in the Grotto of Catullus is the ruin of a Roman villa with good views over the lake from its gardens. The lords of Verona held the Scaliger castle here beside the bridge (13th century; open all year round; closed Mon) and its high tower and battlements make an impressive outline. The

Lake Garda

streets are narrow and atmospheric with arcades and there are two notable churches. Restaurants recommended include the **Grifone** (030-916097) with a terrace on the lake, and **Piccolo Castello** (030-916138) close to the castle with lake fish on the menu. Both reasonable.

From Sirmione go along the narrow promontory to turn left towards Colombare and eventually **PESCHIERA** at the south-eastern corner of the lake. This small town at the mouth of the Mincio has its original ramparts; a restaurant is **Piccolo Mondo** (045-7550025) with fish a speciality and local wines (not cheap). Follow the road to Lazise north along the lake. The scenery is not yet very attractive, yet **LAZISE** is worth noting — it has a castle and a Venetian customhouse (for we are now in the Veneto) as well as the ruins of its ramparts. Go on to **BARDOLINO**, the home of a very good red wine and with the remnants of a castle and a tiny and very ancient church — S. Zeno. This is also the name of one of Verona's finest churches, and if you elect to stay in this spellbinding city of Veneto, the east side of the lake is easily reached at Peschiera, Lazise or Cisano.

The hills become more obvious as you drive towards **GARDA**, an ancient town on a bay — the queen of a son of Charlemagne was held prisoner in its castle and you can visit the ruins which are now minimal. For a fantastic view over the lake go on to Cape S. Virgilio, following the road as it curves to the west from Garda. It is a beautiful headland with a villa (Guarienti) and among the ancient cypresses the little church of S. Virgilio — an excellent picnic spot. The road continues to **TORRI DEL BENACO** with its impressive 14th-century castle. There is a summer resort in the hills above, **S. ZENO DI MONTAGNA**, with fine views, after you have tackled its steep and twisting road, and in the harbour of

Torri del Benaco are picturesque houses and a regular ferry service across to **MADERNO**. [This is the direction of the route, but if you have plenty of time then you can drive right around the lake from here, heading north and then traversing Riva del Garda at the head of the lake to return along a dramatic route on the west shore to Maderno. This little town is charming and has fine views from S. Maria di Gaino 3km away. There are the ruins of a vast Gonzaga villa and, near the landing stage, an ancient church. A worthwhile extension is to **TOSCALANO** a bit to the north where there are walks in the valley of the same name.]

Drive south towards Salo, passing through **GARDONE RIVIERA** with its villas and parks. Along with **FASANO RIVIERA**, is has a particularly mild climate, and together they offer a good start for walks in the nearby hills. There is a museum to the poet d'Annunzio in Gardone — he died here in 1938. At **SALO** pause and enjoy the view of the Island of Garda. There is a fine Gothic duòmo and a famous library, the Biblioteca Anteneo. Here was born Gaspara de Salo, the maker of the first true violin. On towards Desenzano del Garda on 572, turning left to explore lakeside villages along the road towards San Felice del Benaco and on towards **MANERBA** where there are museums, horse-riding and a swimming pool. Rejoin 572 at Moniga del Garda and continue to **DESENZANO** where there is a Roman villa and the ruins of a castle on the hill. Lake ferries leave from here. The church has a Last Supper by Tiepolo. The road follows the lake to Colombare where the turning left for Sirmione is found.

3 THE ITALIAN RIVIERA
(Liguria)

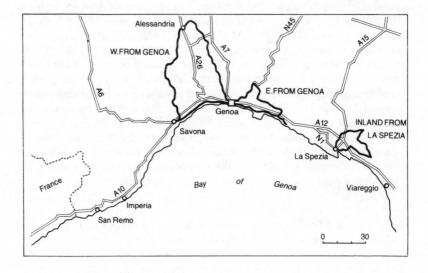

'Green hills enclose a hundred bays, scalloped with sand and kissed by turquoise sea. Can I keep far from such a paradise on earth?' Paradise indeed it must have seemed in the 19th century, for tourists puffing down the new railways into France's southern coasts and Italy's supremely beautiful Riviera which stretches from Menton at the border to just beyond La Spezia along the wide bay of Genoa. Now it has become regrettably too popular with much unsupervised building and a great deal of pollution. Yet the magic still lingers in the golden air, spring comes early, and the vegetation seems to riot as much as grow; it is as lush and exotic as a Caribbean island. On one visit I spent hours walking beneath the flowering trees of the resort of Bordighera, much admired by the English and a literary set including Ronald Firbank, an appropriate spot for that genius of fantasy and atmosphere. There are many places to stay, a vast variety of hotels and guest houses, but be advised — stay away from the main roads if you can, they can be very noisy. Food is also a high priority for visitors, and it is usually very good but beware the establishments that have decided to cater more for the Germans or the Scandinavians, where the light Italian touch has been substituted by heavier foods which they hope will suit the Teutonic tummies, so much on display. Two of the routes in this region use Genoa as a base — it is an under-valued city — too many flash by imagining it to be a sort of Liverpool-on-the-Mediterranean. Go into the town and you will find why it was known in medieval times as La Superba.

GENOA (Italian GENOVA; pop: 810,000) was rival to Venice until struck down at the battle of Chiogga in 1380. Still, she continued to do well even under a parade of foreign masters, and many of her great houses were built in the 16th and 17th centuries. There are numerous palazzi, art galleries and fine buildings, though often badly cared for it's true. A long and leisurely walk should take you along Via Balbi and its continuation, the Via Garibaldi. There is a palace every few paces, and many can be visited — others are offices or commercial enterprises such as banks, but the courtyard and decorations are usually on view. From the Columbus monument on Piazza Acquaverde (other native sons were Paganini — his violin is on show at Palazzo Tursi — and Mazzini, one of the architects of the Risorgimento), you can see Palazzo Reale (fine interior décors), Palazzo Bianco (state art gallery), Palazzo Tursi (fine courtyard with loggias), Palazzo Rosso (Genoese painters) and Palazzo Balbi (elegant entrance), to name but a few. There are many churches (just one: San Matteo, the chapel of the Doria family, dating from the 12th century) and the old town is full of fascinating buildings (towards the port, still the most important in Italy and always busy). Little alleys are known as *carugi* and there are many steep and even stepped streets in Genoa, since the city sits on a shelf between the hills and the sea. There are excellent shops and markets (good for picnic shopping — try the ones along the quay) and specialities at the local restaurants almost always include *pesto*, a subtle green sauce made of pine-nuts crushed with garlic and fresh basil.

There are many excursions possible by bus and train from the capital of Liguria and the autostrade connections from all points are very good. Genoa is also a busy ferry terminal with regular services not only to Sicily and Sardinia but also to points on the African continent and to the Spanish ports of Malaga, Barcelona and Porto Torres. A regular boat trip may be made around the port, taking one hour, from near the Stazione Marittima, and giving you a good impression of the size and import of Genoa as a port today.

While in the city you can, if you are feeling well-off, stay at one of the great alberghi of Italy — the **Colombia Hotel** (010-252061), run by CIGA, and right by the railway station. Even if you can't afford the bedrooms, a visit to the splendid art deco restaurant is well worth the expense — the cooking is splendid.

East from Genoa

1 day or longer/105km

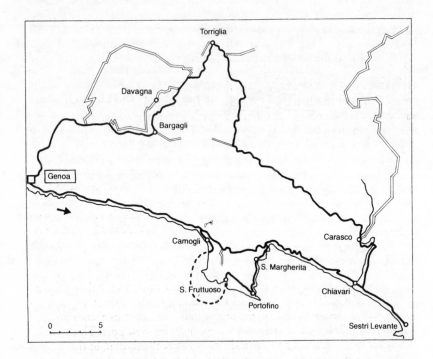

You should leave Genoa by the coast road towards Nervi (Rte 1, although there are extensions from it worth exploring, such as the road down to **BOGLIASCO**, about 10km along, one of several local beach resorts, but, like Nervi, now a part of the Genoese surburban sprawl.) **NERVI** would also make a good base for a stopover, for there are good hotels and a summer ballet festival at the theatre and delightful garden walks as well as two museums. Nervi is the first main resort along the Riviera di Levante (the arm of the coast east of Genoea: opposite and on the other side of the city is the Riviera del Ponente stretching to France) and it has a fine wide promenade along the cliffs: orange and lemon trees scent the air. A little farther on are **SORI** and **RECCO** (about 20km) both small and attractive seaside resorts with beaches; the latter much rebuilt after World War II bombing raids (the target was the railway connection across viaducts; it has a modern church) and now noted for clock-making. Follow road signs here for **CAMOGLI**, right down to the sea. This little fishing port has arcaded streets and a popular festival is held on the first Sunday in August when a fleet of boats sets out for Stella Maris day.

[From this charming town you can make a romantic excursion by boat and on foot to **PUNTA CHIAPPA** for the fantastic sea views or better still to **SAN FRUTTUOSO**, where you would be forgiven if

28

Seafood cultivation

you abandoned the rest of the route and stayed for the day — it is an idyllic village on a tiny beach, backed by an ancient monastery; a simple café provides food and drink for a visit to this village, which can only be reached by sea or on foot (well marked paths lead on to Rapallo via Sta Margherita or the fashionable **PORTOFINO**, where the rich loll on smart white ships and all the shops around the picturesque harbour seem to be smart boutiques).]

This unusual square-shaped peninsula is known as Monte di Portofino and is scheduled as a nature park. There are fine views from **PORTOFINO VETTA**, reached by road from Ruta, just beyond Camogli as you head towards **RAPALLO**. Rapallo is one of the best-known resorts of the Riviera and, like its neighbour, **SANTA MARGHERITA LIGURE**, still has a smart aspect and a sense of sophistication in its restaurants and hotels, but again new construction has somewhat blurred its attractions, especially the new port. This was the home for many years of the wit and satirist, Max Beerbohm, at the Villino Chiara. Rapallo has the good fortune to have a climate that is sheltered and attracts visitors year-round.

The road onwards is distinguished by its sharp bends (some alleviated now with a tunnel) and small valleys. At **CHIAVARI**, a town beside the Entella river, you will find a sand beach and also much charm. Arcaded streets and palm-lined avenues give it a pleasing air. Take the road to the left towards Carasco, unless you wish to make a detour via Lavagna (across the bridge) and the 7km on to the charming and well-situated **SESTRI LEVANTE**. It also has a good beach and, being situated on a little peninsula, actually has two bays and many attractions. There are fine buildings and parks and an art gallery (Pinacotèca Rizzi) as well as a wide selection of hotels. You could continue on from here to La Spezia, but the coast road is still under construction and most of the drive would be inland.

At Carasco you can choose to explore far up the valley of the Sturla Torrente to **SANTO STEFANO D'AVETO** above the Aveto valley — a resort in summer and good for skiing in winter. Our present route takes us left up the 225 towards Cigagna along the valley of the Lavagna. About 6km beyond this village look for signs for and follow a winding road (N45) up to **TORRIGLIA**, beyond the ridge and in the valley of the river Trebbia. A pretty resort with castle and information centre. The road beyond, going towards Montebruno, will take you along hairpin bends and some lovely scenery down along little populated valleys as far as Piacenza. (Look for **BOBBIO** if you continue on this route through mountainous country along the N45. This little settlement has a fine Romanesque church and Irish connections — the tomb of Saint Columba is here in the crypt; the missionary from the green island founded the abbey here in the 7th century, just before his death. The tiny museum of the church has an ancient Roman vessel with a figure in sharp relief as well as carvings from the original church.)

Heading south from Torriglia, take the backroad via Obbi and rejoin the N45 at the point where it ascends to the Passo della Scoffera about 700m up. Continue down the valley (taking the very tortuous road to the right via Davagna if you like a driving challenge) to Bargagli whence the 45 will take you the remaining 20-odd km to Genoa. An alternative route, before crossing the pass, could take you right on the 226 along the valley of the Laccio to Montoggio, where there are camping sites and information offices. An equally winding and narrow road with hairpin bends at its junction with the 45 at Doria will take you on to the centre of Genoa.

West from Genoa

1-2 days/175km

You may well drive along the western arm of the Italian Riviera from France to Genoa and see the scenery *en route*, for even from the coast-hugging autostrada from Ventimiglia there are wondrous views from the A10, which rides above the old road, the N1. Even so, it would hardly be truthful to call this road a rural one, but in Liguria, with the steep hills pressing down to the sea, leaving only a narrow coastal strip, there seems often to be only just room for the one road. In the strict sense this is a main road — but it *does* offer some of the most ravishing views to be found in all Italy and no one visiting Genoa should fail to drive along the Riviera di Ponente facing the rising sun across the Bay of Genoa. A string of pretty resorts, some famous and some hardly known at all, greets the traveller but in summer, of course, it can be fearfully congested as holidaymakers descend on their favourite crescent of sea-washed sand.

The route from Genoa takes you past the airport towards Savona, passing the town of **PEGLI** about 10km from the city. This is a popular all-year resort with a beach set against a curtain of pine-clad hills. Near the station is the principal park with the Villa Doria, now a naval museum (open every day except Sun and Mon) and containing a portrait of Christopher Columbus. Truly palatial is the Villa Durazzo-Pallavicini in a stylish park carved out of the hillside and filled with all sorts of early 19th-century garden conceits including Chinese temples, medieval castles and underground lakes. Great fun but watch out for the water-games! In the villa itself is an archaeological museum with finds from Liguria — open as for the naval museum. There are fine walks and views. Inland from Pegli, up twisting mountain roads, are several fine churches such as the one at Acquasanta. (The Santuario, this 17th-century church, was the scene of a dynastic marriage between Marie Cristina of Savoy and the king of the Two Sicilies in 1832.)

Passing on the N1 you now start to leave the sprawl of Genoese suburbs and at Voltri, an industrial town, you cross the river Leiro.

[Here you can make a detour to ascend the winding road towards Mele (N456) to **CAMPO LIGURIA** high in the hills to view its castle, and continue along a small circular route through the mountains via Rossiglione (right if you wish to explore a short dead end road up the valley of the Berlino) then 1½km on turn left towards Montecalvo and **TIGLIETO** with its fine church and information centre. Return to the N456 past Monte Praioli and rejoin at the Turchino Pass to go back to Voltri.]

Continue along the N1 to **ARENZANO**, with its seawater baths and beach, to **VARAZZE**, a charming old town with ramparts and, oddly preserved, a 10th-century façade (Sant'Ambrogio). There are groves of oranges and in the hills beyond, up yet another narrow mountain road, the sanctuary of Monte Beigua, high on a lonely hilltop.

Ligurian village

Celle Ligure is another resort just before the road enters the environs of **SAVONA**, untidy and depressing at first sight, but push on to the centre where you will find grand Baroque churches and several small treasures such as medieval tower houses (near the quay, heavily damaged in World War II) and a terrace of charming 1930s houses looking over the harbour, along with a medieval watch tower. The main street, handsomely arcaded Via Paleocapa, goes from the station to the harbour.

From here you can continue along the N1 for a considerable distance before you reach the border. You will pass through such famous towns as **ALASSIO**, which has beaches, promenades and fine gardens as well as a stronghold, the Torrione, constructed as protection against pirates; **IMPERIA**, a pleasant town astride a river with a busy trade in olive oil; **SAN REMO** with its grand hotels and golf and race courses, the largest resort on the Italian Riviera and possessing an atmospheric old centre which is known as La Pigna. There is a carnival every year and flower markets serving one of the principal industries of this coast. Needless to say San Remo has fine restaurants; not all expensive as is **Giannino's** on the Lugomare Trento facing the sea. Try **Silvestro's** on Verezzo Cava (0184-559066) for bargain meals in the quality bracket. Farther along the N1 you come to beautiful **BORDIGHERA**, a long-time favourite with British visitors and most popular in winter for its mild climate. In the middle of the old town (Capo Ampeglio) is the Spianata del Capo with very good views. The town has the right to supply palmfronds to the Vatican at Easter. The Via dei Colli along the hills gives good views over the coast. Last is **VENTIMIGLIA**, where there are many narrow streets clustered with tall houses, and a fortified wall. There is a flower market and interesting churches here, while outside the town and open daily are the Giardini Hanbury, botanic gardens founded over a century ago.

There is no good alternative road back from the entry point to France at Grimaldi, since roads inland tend to follow river valleys and are tortuous and slow to drive along, so you will either need to retrace your journey back to Genoa or take the A10 autostrada, which runs through the hills with many tunnels along its length and does give an overview down to the coast of the route you have already traversed — a kind of bird's eye effect at times.

Returning, you could take a turn into the Piedmont region and a great deal of fine mountain scenery. In addition there are many tiny roads to explore and enquiries at local tourist offices will supply information: for example — the folklore feast in July at Loano and a spaghetti museum at Pontedassio just up in the hills beyond Imperia!

The road north from Albisola is the N334 towards Stella (the junction is about 4km east of Savona) and **ALBISOLA** itself is worth a stop — the birthplace of a pope, Julius II, who commissioned Michelangelo to build an ornate tomb, and also a famous centre for pottery since the Middle Ages. Albisola is actually two small towns on either side of the river Riobasco which parallels the road as far as Stella and peters out before the Colle del Giovo, at which point the road descends towards **SASSELLO**, an agreeable mountain resort. Here you could either take a small road going east towards Rossiglione, or continue on to the ranges on the border of Liguria and Piedmont. The former will take you back to the coast via the N456 (already described); the latter goes on towards Acqui Terme (signposted) along a good road (a branch to the left at the Piedmont border goes towards Pareto and an alternative route north from **SPIGNO MONFERRATO**, where there is an ancient abbey with fine frescoes.)

ACQUI TERME (pop: 22,000), as its name suggests, was and still is a spa (you will see it as you enter the town) where there are treatments for many ailments including rheumatism, gout and arthritis with mud baths at the central spa building. Interesting is the fountain, known as the Boiling One (La Bollente) since its waters warmed from the sulphurous depths are at a temperature of 75°. This would be a pleasing place to stay, especially if you wish for treatments — the spa is open year round. There is a public garden with a ruined castle and a fine Romanesque duòmo with a 13th-century campanile. A good restaurant in Acqui is the **Parisio** (0144-53736) and the family have now another at **Carlo Parisio** (0144-56650) which is less expensive.

Going from this town on the river Bormida (there is also a part of a Roman aqueduct on the other side) towards Alessandria, the road descends in leisurely manner along the Bormida. **ALESSANDRIA** is very much a town of the late 18th century in style, a centre for local industry and agriculture. Continue on south towards Genoa, passing the battlefield at **MARENGO** where Napoleon overcame the Austrian armies in 1800, commemorated with a column. There are roads to explore on either side of the valley of the infant Po river. After a distance of about 20km from Alessandria, and just after cutting the A20 autostrada, you come to **POZZOLO** with its castle, and a sign towards **NOVI LIGURE**, with its impressive medieval tower over a modern town — here was fought the battle against the French, prior to the victory at Marengo. From Novi take the rural road to the right, rather than the N35 to Genoa. Follow signs for **GAVI** and in about 10km you will arrive at this pretty town on the Torrente Lemme. There is a handsome 13th-century church. On towards Voltaggio, the road gives good views especially when it has crossed the hills and headed down towards Liguria after the pass at La Bocchetta. Up to this point you have been traversing the Cappane di Marcarolo, a large natural park on the border of Piemonte, one of more than a dozen in this region. The road descends swiftly to Pontedecimo, where it rejoins the N35 and an easy drive down the valley to Genoa.

Inland from La Spezia

1 day/about 110km

The port of **LA SPEZIA** is sheltered by the two arms that embrace the Golfo della Spezia, facing south and overlooked by pleasant resort towns.

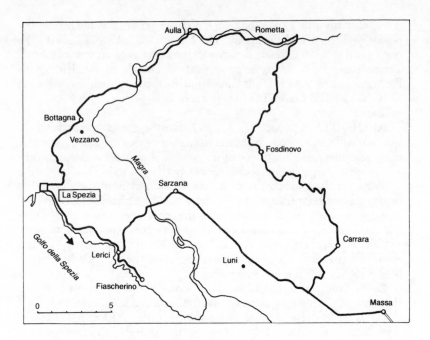

It is an important naval centre and a provincial capital (pop: 124,000) and the town faces the water, backed by mountains. There are good parks, complete with orange and palm trees, and a statue of Garibaldi, overlooking the sea. There is a naval arsenal you can visit (apply for a permit, taking a passport for identification) and an old citadel, while appropriate to this naval town is a naval museum (open every day) which shows the maritime history of the area with an array of instruments and weapons. There is also an important archaeological museum in the town, the Lunense Library, with many items from the digs at Luni (Roman and earlier.) Open every day including Sunday mornings. The cathedral has been rebuilt: there is a large della Robbia in one of the aisles — the Coronation of the Virgin.

From La Spezia take the road south towards Lerici along the coast, passing through **S. TERENZO** where there is a castle, a fishing village once the home of the poet Shelley at Casa Magni. It was from here that he commenced the voyage to Livorno (English: Leghorn) resulting in his death, and the house situated on a headland is now a museum. A little farther and you are in **LERICI**, a year-round resort offering watersports to the athletically inclined. Both Dante and Petrarch stayed at the 13th-century castle and the charming little chapel of Sts Martin and Christopher should be visited. Try the well-recommended **Conchiglia** restaurant (0187-967334), lots of good fish dishes. [If you wish, continue on the (dead end) coast road to **FIASCHERINO**, once the home of D. H. Lawrence, and the dramatically placed **TELLARO**, a medieval village

34

Leaning Tower of Pisa

perched above the sea. Or, another route from Lerici goes south towards **AMAGLIA**, a longish and wandering road passing through fine scenery as it ambles down the peninsula, ending at this little town with its ancient castle. From here cross the Magra river to rejoin the route at N1, about 2km beyond the autostrada.]

The main road from Lerici strikes over the hills and then down to **SARZANA** (N331), which still posseses ancient town gates and some of its defensive fortifications. The cathedral is worth a visit. Built during two centuries, it was finished in the 15th and contains an ancient painting of the crucifix and gilded vaults in the choir. From Sarzana follow signs for

35

the N1 and then head south towards Massa. On the way are the scattered ruins of the Etruscan and later Roman city of **LUNI** — a thriving port and once very important town laid waste by sickness (marsh-born malaria) and also the attacks of pirates. There is a small museum (closed Mon) with remains of the once great settlement. The N1 crosses into Tuscany here, and almost at once you see the white quarries in the sides of the Apuan Alps — about 4km after the regional line turn left along an indicated road to the town of Carrara.

[To the right is the Marina di Carrara and, ahead, the town of **MASSA**, once capital of a duchy and still containing the impressively sited Rocca, a castle of the Malaspina family. Its one-time ducal palace, 17th century, unabashedly Baroque, has an elegant courtyard. If you continue even further along the N1 you will come eventually to **PISA**, with its famous Campo Santo and the grouping of the Duòmo, the elegant Baptistery and the Leaning Tower (campanile) clustered in spectacular architectural effect. Pisa is a very useful centre for touring Tuscany and it has a remarkably complete medieval centre with many churches. It is about 45km from Massa and its airport serves Florence as well as the Pisan area. Also along the route are **PIETRASANTA**, heavily bombarded in World War II, and possessing a beautiful central square, the Piazza del Duòmo; and the popular and crowded seaside resort of **VIAREGGIO**, with a wide beach of good sand and numerous hotels and restaurants. Viarreggio is surrounded with pine woods and gardens and it is also a winter resort. Its double promenade, a road and a walk-way, faces the sea and the port with an ancient watch tower.]

CARRARA, the famous centre for white marble, was frequently visited by Michelangelo. His house, where he supposedly stayed when he came here to purchase marble, can be seen on the main square. There is a museum in the castle (Belli Arti) and the duòmo is a pleasing mixture of Romanesque and Gothic. The quarries can be visited (bus from the town to Colonnata), high up in the hills and surrounded by splendid wild scenery — afterwards you may care to seek out the many small workshops in Carrara, and there is also a museum dedicated to the sculpturing and working of marble on the Viale XX Settembre.

From Carrara look for the N446 dir winding up towards the village of Gragnana and up to the little settlement of **FOSDINOVO** where in a fold of the hills can be seen the castle of the Malaspina (a little left of the junction with the main N446). Follow this road north through lonely mountain scenery until it reaches the main N63 near Rometta.

Turn left and head towards **AULLA.** This town, situated in a steep-sided valley of the Magra river, is at a road junction and the autostrada parallels the N63 along the river. Aulla has a striking fort, Brunella, dating from the 16th century. Turn left, following the signs for La Spezia. At Caprigliola turn right onto the N330, a distance of about 7km. This will take you across the now-wide valley of the Magra to **VEZZANO**. Here are numerous interesting buildings in the settlement (on a narrow backroad from Bottagna at the intersection of the N330) and also on down the road to La Spezia once you have crossed the hills.

Fishermen might like to note there is good sport to be had along the Magra where it widens out and becomes slower on its way down to the sea. You finish this route in the suburbs just east of La Spezia and turn right along the N1 to enter the rear of the town.

4 THE VENETO
(Veneto, Friuli-Venezia Giulia and Trentino-Alto Adige)

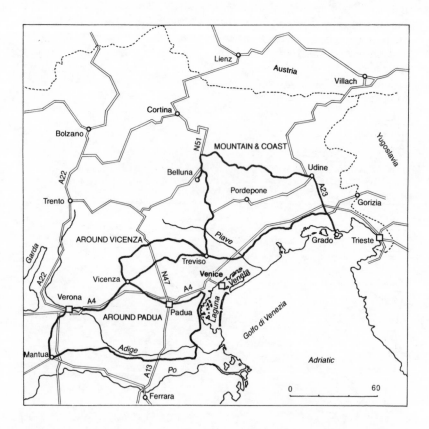

As its name suggests, the Veneto is essentially to do with Venice — the proud republic mushrooming on the marshy islands of the sea to become one of the greatest powers of medieval Europe. Now, Venice, or Venezia as she is known in Italy, is a shadow of her former greatness, and a small city compared to the urban sprawl of many another Italian centre; yet the Queen of the Adriatic still has a hauntingly beautiful atmosphere. The dominance of Venice over the sea extended to the mainland and nearby towns soon came under her sway, making the area known today as the Veneto, and still marked everywhere with the proudly posturing Lion of St Mark. Venice, however, does not make a good centre for driving since you will have to leave your car at the vast garage at her gates and take to the water to get to a hotel, and accommodation in the city is hard to find. These routes are planned around the satellites of 'La Serenissima', with possibilities of daytime visits to the city. They also extend in one route out of the Veneto and into the mountains and across to the city of Trieste. The country around Venice is flat and open, beyond the waters of the famous lagoon, but rises in the north towards the castellated heights of the Dolomites and the hills around Lake Garda in the west. It is an area that is filled with enchantment, from the tall campanili of the churches standing in the countryside like brick exclamation marks, to the grand villas of Palladio close to Vicenza. Often the suburbs of towns are ragged and dusty, but the centres are marvellous, and almost every town will have a treasure — a museum, a building, a view. The food is varied, but naturally fish comes high on menus, and there are many local specialities to sample as well as Veneto wines.

Around Vicenza

1 or 2 days/about 130km plus city walk/from Vicenza

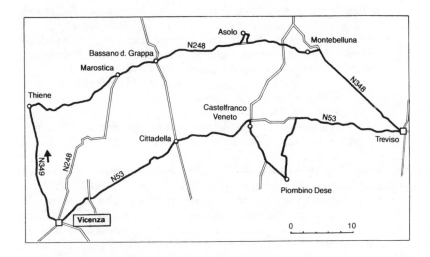

L'angelo messaggero nell'Italia liberata dai Goti
(Dedication by il Trissino upon giving the humble sculptor Andrea della Gondola the resounding name of Palladio)

This route is more urban than rural, but I make no apologies, for the treasures of one of the world's greatest architects, Andrea Palladio, are in concentration here. The influence of this great Italian, in fact born in Padua in 1508, is evident all around the world, with houses built in 'Palladian style' from the USA to Australia. Britain possesses Palladian influence in many of its country houses but to see the glory of Palladio's genius you must travel to Vicenza and stay for a few days in order to view his works at leisure. Here, in the surrounding country of softly rounded hills, he built his great country villas, most of them open to visitors at certain times; others require invitations, but even arriving unannounced can be fruitful — I recall Swiss friends ringing a bell beside a board which indicated quite plainly the villa was closed. A beseeching talk to the porter, a small tip, and we were rewarded with a private visit!

Vicenza fell early to the thrall of Venice and the Lion of St Mark is everywhere apparent. Although not open and easy in plan as is its neighbour Verona, the city makes an excellent base to tour from and is quickly reached from Milan or Venice along the ubiquitous but undeniably handy autostrada.

The town plan of **VICENZA** (pop: 105,000) shows a tight web of narrow streets radiating across waterways to the roughly circular road marking the old walls and defences. Here can be seen a half-score of buildings from all periods of Palladio's life. It is of course best to walk rather than drive, so wear comfortable shoes and appropriate clothes — the weather can be cold in the autumn and winter, for in the distance you can see the snowy peaks of the Alps. Start at the Piazza dei Signori in the centre of the city where next to the elegant brick clocktower rises the **Basilica Palladiana**. This is one of the architect's earliest works and is essentially a shell covering the old Gothic *palazzo della ragione*. It is a remarkably clever construction, however, for the building is not regular and Palladio has devised cunning ways of ensuring his immaculate sense of proportion in the double, wide-arched loggia that embraces the old city hall. It can be visited at any time — or view it from a table at one of the open-air cafés on the square.

Next, visit the later **Loggia del Capitaniato** nearby, a sort of very grand, and rather florid, porch begun in 1570, ten years before the architect's death. Continue up to the corner of the Via San Gaetano and the Corso Palladio where you will find the **Palazzo Thiene**. This heavily rusticated, two-storey palace is an early adaptation of the architect's, and a little farther down you can see a later work, the **Palazzo Barbaran del Porto**, dating from the same period as the Loggia. The **Palazzo Valmarana** on the same street is grandly classical, begun in 1565, and like so many of his works showing the results of his sojourn in Rome. Continue along the Corso Palladio and turn left at the end to find the curious, narrow **Palazzo da Porto Breganze**, which may have been a collaboration with the other grand architect of the Veneto of the time, Vincenzo Scamozzi.

Retracing your steps to the Corso Tra Porti and turning left you will find the **Palazzo da Porto Festa**, built after his first Roman visit in 1541

Teatro Olimpico, Vicenza

when he was in his early thirties. Its recessed windows and stone balconies on the first floor are particularly attractive, and the building is contrasted with an earlier Gothic high-windowed palazzo next door.

An early building, attributed to other hands for many years, is the elegant **Casa Civeno Trissino** farther down this street, but best of all are two Palladian works at the end of the Corso Palladio off the Piazza Matteotti. Here are the lovely open loggias of the **Palazzo Chiericati** with its row of statues along the roof line, and the unique **Teatro Olympico**. If you see nothing else, it must be this wooden theatre which dates from Palladio's final year of life, 1580. A marvel of eye-teasing effect. There are many other aspects of this pleasing, small city to enjoy, and good shopping and restaurants, too. A couple to note: **Allo Scudo di Francia**, a reasonably priced family place (0444-26684) and at the entrance to the city the **Motel Agip** (0444-564711). There are many places to stay in Vicenza, besides motels, especially around the central piazza, where strolling before or after dinner is a delight.

This tour takes in most of the great Palladian villas in the area, and is therefore somewhat weighted in favour of architecture buffs, but for those just wanting a scenic drive there is much to enjoy in these low hills with views to the north of mountains. Start from Vicenza towards Trento on the road towards **CALDOGNO** on the N349. Here you can glimpse, but unfortunately not visit, the Villa Caldogno of 1570. (All villas are by Palladio, unless otherwise credited here.) Continue on through **VILLAVERLA** where there are country houses by Scamozzi and Pizzocaro, towards **THIENE** beyond a confluence of highways where you will find a 15th-century castellated villa (visits spring to autumn, including the charming contemporary chapel: in the Colleoni castle are paintings and frescoes). From Thiene you can make excursions to **SCHIO** a textile town with an 18th-century cathedral, or up towards the mountains and **ASIAGO**, a smart resort for both summer and winter visitors with good sports facilities and hotels. There is a large cemetery of victims of the 1918 Battle of Asiago, both British and Italian, and also an astrophysical observatory belonging to Padua University. Asiago is modern, but the air is excellent and there are fine walks.

Continue on the main route from Thiene to Marostica, enjoying good views as you go. **MAROSTICA** is a medieval settlement with buildings on two levels — two castles and walls with impressive ramparts. If you don't wish to climb Monte Pausolino to the upper castle, you can enjoy a view of this 14th-century stronghold of the Scaliger family from the main piazza where every two years a human chess game is played (even years). This *partita a scacchi* takes place in early September. Go on to Bassano del Grappa although an earlier excursion just before Marostica can be made to the two villas at **LONEDO DI LUGO** — the Villa Godi is a striking early work (open several days a week) and has a modern art museum and the Villa Piovene has its Palladian work masked by later 18th-century additions (admission to garden).

At **BASSANO DEL GRAPPA** (pop: 35,000) there is a most fascinating monument to Palladio — a wooden bridge offering a covered crossing of the Brenta. It has been much rebuilt yet retains the architect's 17th-century design and can be seen well from the ponte Vittoria. Bassano was the home of the painter Jacopo da Ponte (known as Bassano) and there are works of his in the *museo civico*. The arcaded streets are a pleasant feature of the town, and the picturesque Piazza Monte Vecchio should be visited. There are ceramic shops, and wrought ironware is also made, but most famous are the fat brown *porcini*, mountain mushrooms, which can be purchased fresh in season or else dried.

From Bassano take N47 north looking for signs for 248 going directly east towards Montebelluna. Half-way towards this town you will come to **ASOLO**, a town of great distinction and charm which was a favourite of Browning who set some of his poems there (*Pippa Passes*). His son is buried in the churchyard, as is Eleonora Duse. This was the town of the Queen of Cyprus, Catherine Cornaro, and she lived in the castello which may be visited. Here she created in the early 16th century a theatre, now at the Ringling Brothers Museum in Asolo, Florida. There are pretty streets and squares, a 15th-century *palazzo comunale* and paintings in the cathedral. There are several fine restaurants, so maybe you might plan lunch here or even stay over! (CIGA have a splendid historic hotel here.) Try **Locana 2 Mori** (0423-52256) for bargain meals with specialities of *funghi* and the oddly-named **Charly's One** (0423-52201), where despite the attempt to create an English pub atmosphere, the food is very good.

Not far from Asolo at the approach to Montebelluno is **MASER**, where you will find one of the most entrancing of villas, the Villa Barbaro, standing in a great theatrical parade against low hills and trees. There are marvellous gardens and grottoes with a temple, also by Palladio. Inside are spectacular frescoes by Veronese and elegant plasterwork — this is a place to savour and enjoy, with a walk afterwards perhaps along the frontal arcade and a visit to the Carriage Museum in the grounds. A delightful little Baroque church at the entrance to the villa has a classical portico. South of here is **FANZOLO**, where you will find the Villa Emo, an unusual example of the kind of 'grand farm' effect where the landowner lived on his estate and wanted a house that kept its feet on the land — note the grand staircase and the impressive sweep of its arcades.

From Maser continue to **MONTEBELLUNA,** a modern town on a hill with a handsome 17th-century church.

Take 348, the road towards **TREVISO** (pop: 100,000), to arrive at this city on water, an old town and a provincial capital badly damaged in World War II, yet well restored. The town is built over the branches of the river Sile and tributaries, and results in a charming canal-like feeling with arcaded streets of houses along narrow throroughfares. The town is roughly oblong in shape with near-complete fortifications. There are many interesting buildings — a 12th-century baptistery and campanile, a cathedral, several impressive churches and a *Palazzo del Podesta*, with tall tower, actually a 19th-century edifice, in old style. But Treviso's charm lies in its streets and squares, busy and crowded, especially the central Piazza dei Signori. Good places to eat and many small shops. An easy excursion from here could take you down to **VENICE** (Italian: VENEZIA) for there are swift and frequent trains and with the difficulty of finding good accommodation on the lagoon, a stopover in Treviso could be very attractive. The station in Venice is right on the Grand Canal and the little *vaporetti* will take you swiftly and moderately cheaply to destinations through the city travelling on the water.

From Treviso take N53 towards Vicenza, via **PIOMBINO DESE** which is reached from this road by heading down towards Padua. Here is a simple, striking villa with a double-pillared portico, framed by tall trees —

View of Venice

the Villa Cornaro, built for a Doge of Venice. There are fine stuccoes within. At **CASTELFRANCO VENETO** you are greeted with a statue of its most famous citizen — the painter Giorgione. The old town is surrounded with walls and a moat, and to see Giorgione's work go to the 18th-century cathedral where his great picture 'Madonna and Child with Saints' can be seen in a chapel. There is a castle, and pleasant walks around this small town. Castelfranco stands just off the main road. Continue back towards Vicenza by way of **CITTADELLA** at the junction of N47. Here you will find a fortified town of the Paduans with its walls making a picturesque sight. N53 continues across the edge of the wide Venetian plain to arrive at Vicenza.

Having returned to Vicenza, you may care to make a local excursion to view the famous Villa Rotonda and Monte Berico. This is an easy walk, but you can drive or take local bus services. There is a grand basilica at Monte Berico with a covered approach and a Gothic cloister. Fine views of both Vicenza itself and the Villa Rotonda (or Villa Capra), which can be reached by taking a side-road past the Villa Valmarana dei Narni (because of the stone dwarfs on its walls) which is by Muttoni and has frescoes by Tiepolo father and son. Although you cannot go into the Villa Rotonda, the surroundings are very pleasant and the villa itself a very impressive architectural ensemble on its hilltop.

Around Padua

1 or 2 days/about 250km/from Padua

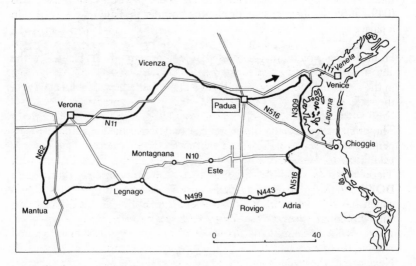

It may not seem an obvious choice for a centre to stay, but **PADUA** (Italian: PADOVA; pop: 250,000) is a city with a lot to offer once you have penetrated the ugly suburbs and factory districts clustered close to its ring road. The old city has much charm, with arcaded and elegant buildings and the exotic outline of the pilgrimage church of St Antony, and is threaded with the tributaries of the river Bacchiglione. It is a city of art, and a visit to see the famous Giotto frescoes in the Cappella Scrovegni is a 'must' — they line the little church almost like cartoon strips in brilliant colours. But to this master must also be added the incomparable Mantegna (whose major work was lost, alas, in a bombing raid of 1944) and the amazing sculptures of Donatello. His statue of the condottiere Gattamelata is a splendid piece (Piazza del Santo) and the altar in S. Antonio is also his work. Mantegna's work can still be glimpsed in the Eremetani church, restored and presented in recovered fragments after the bombing, but it is a sad shadow.

The centre of Padua is the Piazza Cavour, and the famous and very old university. Here you can see in the museum the oldest anatomical theatre in the world, and many famous doctors have gained their degrees here. The *palazzo della ragione* is a vast construction of the 13th century, and it now covers a fascinating market. Many fine buildings cluster around Piazza delle Erbe and the Piazza delle Frutte. The duòmo itself was originally reconstructed to designs of Michelangelo, but the final result is merely heavy. There is, however, a fine Romanesque baptistery with many frescoes. The big church of S. Antonio is much more interesting and for the curiosity seeker there are bizarre reliquaries. After a quick trot around the many churches and buildings, you must pay a visit to the famous **Caffé Pedrocchi** in the centre of the city — a beautiful 19th-century café which is famous throughout Italy. There is a civic museum of note, and a very interesting Botanic Garden with specimen trees — it is reputedly the oldest in Europe. For good eating try **Dotto** (049-25055) — inexpensive; or else the grander **El Toula** (049-26649) in a palace.

From Padua you can go towards Venice across the plain on the autostrada, but much more attractive is the drive along the Brenta canal in the same direction, terminating if you wish in a visit to the great city on the water. Along the canal, reached by turning to the right on 11 towards Dolo, you come to a whole defile of fine villas set in a series of gardens. The atmosphere is marvellous, misted and soft, and an autumn day is perfect for a visit to these grand old ghosts of another era, the country *palazzi* of the Venetian aristocrats. At **STRA** is the Villa Pisani, with Tiepolo frescoes, and usually open to view at set hours. Go on through **DOLO** where there is a good restaurant, **Al Bondante** (041-420745) which has fish dishes in Venetian stle. At **FIESSO D'ARTICO** is the Villa Barbariga of the 18th century, at **MIRA** the Palazzo Foscarini, where Byron lived in 1817. In Mira a local restaurant, family-run and notable, is **Margherita** (041-420879) in a pretty garden on the canal. Next comes the Villa Costanza of the early 18th century (later altered) and then **MALCONTENTA** where the beautiful Villa Foscari by Palladio of 1574 is to be found — open from May to October. At nearby **FUSINA** it is possible to take a boat to Venice. Take a sharp turn and head south along the Venetian lagoon on 309. [This goes ultimately to **CHIOGGIA** — a worthwhile detour, for here you will find a pleasant fishing port and nearby beach and, in the narrow streets of the town, several fine buildings including a marble-lined cathedral; there is a shady terrace beside the Brenta canal, and many small hotels and fish restaurants at **SOTTOMARINA**, the beach suburb.]

There is a good view of Chioggia from the 309 as you cross the Brenta heading towards Cona. Turn to the left on 516 crossing the plain to arrive at **ADRIA**. Here you will find an ancient settlement of Greekish-Etruscan foundation. The city gave its name to the Adriatic — now is is far removed by the extended mouths of the river Po. The Museo Civico has a collection of vases and jewellery and a chariot of iron, dating back to the 4th century BC. From here you could join with one of the routes of the Marche, taking in the Abbey of Pomposa and the superb city of Ferrara, by heading south. This route, however, goes west on 443 to **ROVIGO** (pop: 50,000). This is the principal town of the Polesine, and possesses several good 17th-century constructions and some old parts of the original fortifications. The Palazzo Roncale of 1555 is worth seeking out. **Tre Pini** is a good local restaurant (0425-27111) in a handsome house on the Ferrara side of the town. From Rovigo continue on up the wide flat valley towards Lendinara and eventually the village of **LEGNAGO**. Here was situated one of the Austrian occupying armies' 'quadrilaterals' (or defensive positions) on the banks of the Adige. A private museum of weapons is contained in the Palazzo Fiorini.

[From here you can make an excursion along N10 to **ESTE** where there is a castle in this bastion of the noble Este family, later Dukes of Ferrara. In the large and impressive building is the home of the Atestino museum, with many unusual antiquities as well as prehistoric pieces. The public garden is also within the castle walls, and from the keep there is a good view. The 13th-century church of S. Martino is worth visiting — note the incline of the campanile. Byron and Shelley stayed at the Villa Kenkler. On the way to Este note the little town of **MONTAGNANA** with its ancient walls and gateways all in warm-coloured brick, well worth a stop for exploration — there is a Gothic cathedral.]

Continue from Legnago to Verona, either directly via Bovalone, or you may turn left on N10 at Cerea to visit **MANTUA**. This city (Italian: MANTOVA; pop: 70,000) has many monuments and has a trade in silk. Here were cradled the Gonzaga family and their great palace, the severe Reggia dei Gonzaga, an enormous rambling place which ought to be visited if only to see Mantegna's Camera degli Sposi, the marriage-chamber, where the frescoes are still vibrant and beautiful. Also here, a curiosity, are the apartments of the dwarfs of one of the dukes, and the inlaid wood of the rooms of Isabella d'Este. A restaurant with a view and a dramatic flair is **Rigoletto** (0376-371167), while perhaps the best is **Il Cigno** (0376-327101) which is expensive but very much a 'Mantovano' experience. From Mantua go to Verona on the main road via Villafranca di Verona.

VERONA (pop: 300,000) is a glittering city of great allure, with marvellous views and walks and a series of superb buildings. It makes a wonderful centre for exploration of the Veneto, or, as has been suggested, of Lake Garda. There is much to see and do here, whether you merely sit and watch the people on the busy Piazza Bra, or go to the opera in the Roman amphitheatre, or stroll along pedestrian streets to gaze at the luxuries on show in the shops. Piazza delle Erbe is still a market on the site of the Roman forum and you can gaze up, as many famous people have, at the supposed balcony of Juliet — the young men on the street have a decided look of latter-day Romeos. There is an impressive early duòmo, but best of all is the fantastic 12th-century church of San Zeno. Even if you are bored with churches, this magnificent church, both simple and satisfying, will move you. Restaurants — try **Re Teodorico** (045-49903) or **La Diga** with inventive dishes (045-563194).

From Verona return to Padua on 11, or if time is of the essence, the autostrada E13, both via Vicenza.

Mountain and Coast
1 or 2 days/340km/from Belluno

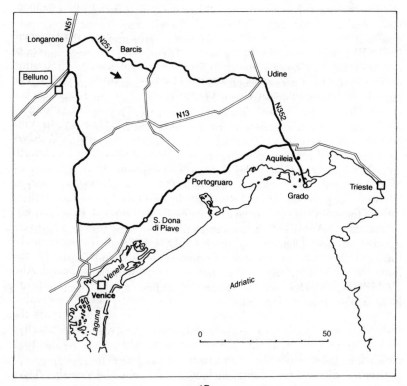

You could base yourself for this route in Treviso, in Conegliano, or even in Udine, or start down from Cortina, but **BELLUNO** (pop: 40,000) is ideal because of its location and its views to the mountains. It is well equipped with hotels and with good places to eat and is also a centre for ski enthusiasts, adding an extra attraction in winter months, though extreme care should be taken on mountain roads then.

The town itself stands at the point where the rivers Ardo and Piave join, clustered along a rocky point and surrounded by mountains. You can climb the 18th-century campanile of the duòmo (much restored after earthquakes) for the view but for the ground-bound there are excellent viewpoints from the 12th-century Rugo Gate and other parts. There is an old town with Renaissance buildings, and modern suburbs. Restaurants include **Al Sasso** on a little square (0437-22424) and characteristic of the region, while **Al Borgo** (0437-24006) is family run with local wines.

From Belluno follow the road over the Ardo, being sure to look back at the prospect of the town. There are striking mountains all around and nearby the huge hydroelectric dam of Piave-S. Croce. At **LONGARONE** you reach the site of a flood caused in 1963 by a landslide into the pent-up waters. Turn right here towards Barcis [although by continuing on the same road a very agreeable detour may be made into the high Dolomites and the popular ski and resort town of **CORTINA D'AMPEZZO**, from which many excursions by car and foot are possible into the mountains, which stand like castellations in the unique configuration of rock found in these ranges. Good hotels and excellent winter sports facilities. On the way stop at **PIEVE DI CADORE**, which was the birthplace of Titian; there is a museum and one of his pictures hangs in the church.]

The Barcis road goes through beautiful mountainous countryside and enter Frivli-Venezia Givlia towards **MANIAGO**, where once steel knives were made for export; now the tamer trade is cutlery. There is a good duòmo with frescoes. South from here, along the side of the Meduna, is **PORDE-NONE**, an industrial city of the Friuli, also damaged by the 1976 'quakes (as was Maniago). There is a handsome main street with painted house fronts and arcades, and the duòmo (closed) has a fine campanile. The rather bizarre *palazzo comunale* has a clocktower. The route from Maniago to Udine may be followed along the minor road through Dignano on its river, or you can stay on the main road (13) from Pordenone passing through Casarsa with to the right **SAN VITO'S** tall campanile. You cross the Tagliamento downstream from Dignano and reach **CODROIPO**, just to the right of the road. This was an important Roman settlement and nearby is the huge Villa Manin, once the home of a Venetian doge, and **CAMPOFORMIDO** on the edges of Udine recalls memories of Napoleon's conquest of the area.

UDINE (pop: 115,000) is a centre of clothmaking and metal foundries. It clusters around its main hill with many of its old streets charmingly arcaded. Its town plan is almost square and it has several fine buildings on the central Piazza della Liberta, including the Loggia del Lionello. The castle hill (shaken in the '76 earthquake and still much closed off) has a gateway by Palladio (the Arco Bollani) and the castle itself is usually in service as a museum. A small place to eat is **All'Antica Maddalena** (0432-25111) or you could try the popular and cheap **Roma** (0432-299358).

From Udine go south towards **PALMANOVA**, reached by turning right onto 352 from the main road (56) to Gorizia on the Yugoslav border. Here you will find a striking fortress of Venetian origin with a hexagonal central court, brick built and with a moat, now dry and with three gates, all built in the 16th century. The duòmo is 17th century, by Longhena. Go below the autostrada to reach **CERVIGNANO DEL FRIULI**, a pleasant small town and a point at which you can, if you wish, turn right to follow the old road to Trieste.

[**TRIESTE** pop: 300,000. This sea port and provincial capital is open and mostly modern, but it has several interesting monuments, not least its cathedral, S. Giusto, which contains a number of styles and periods based on a 5th-century basilica. Climb the campanile for the view. Remnants of Roman buildings are incorporated, including columns, and in the town is preserved the foundations of a theatre. A Roman basilica is marked out before the Castello, which may be visited and which offers good views of the city from its walls. It was founded in the 14th century and much altered by the Austrians. In Trieste the life of the city pulses along the harbour; there are many good restaurants and pleasant cafés. The city was originally the Roman port of Tergeste.]

From Cervignano drive down towards the coast to **GRADO**, a fishing port and resort with a sand beach and spa, and many interesting houses in its narrow-streeted centre. There is an ancient church with mosaics of the 6th century. The neighbouring baptistery and accompanying small church are also very old. In July (1st Sunday) there is a boat procession to the island of **BARBANA**, otherwise regular excursions. The Grado road is also fascinating for **AQUILEIA** on the present mainland. This truly remarkable Roman site on a wide plain is well worth visiting, and it has added fascination because it lingered into the Middle Ages and its basilica is a splendid one dating back to the 4th century and has a large mosaic floor. See also the frescoed crypt. The site itself is for walking visits and there is much to see, although much remains to be excavated. There is also a museum.

Return to Cervignano and travel alongside the sea towards **PORTOGRUARO**, a delightful arcaded town with a leaning tower to its cathedral. Continue towards **S. DONÀ** (perhaps turning off *en route* to see the seaside town of **CAORLE** with good cathedral) where there are fine views north to the mountains as you approach. Shortly after, take the turn right signposted to Treviso; turn north after crossing the autostrada A27 to find N13 to **CONEGLIANO**. This town in the foothills is a centre of wine-growing and from here you can follow well-marked red and white wine routes through pretty low hills, sampling as you go. In the cathedral is a picture by Cima, who was born here and who has links in the town. There is a castle on a hill with good views of the surrounding countryside and in the guild-hall there are numbers of frescoes. The town has good Renaissance houses in Venetian style. Why not eat at a restaurant dedicated to and named after **Cima**? It is modern and spacious and you can try local wines (0438-22648).

Continue north on N13 to **VITTORIO VENETO,** where the Italians finally achieved victory in 1918 — there is a museum of the battle and a monument. The old town is above the industrial section and separate village of Ceneda, and has some very good buildings notably the arcaded houses of the Via Martiri della Liberta and the Piazza Flaminia. The Loggia Serravallese is named after the old village and the 15th-century building is now a museum. In the lower town there is a later Loggia Cenedese.

Go up the ascending N51 to return to Belluno.

5 EMILIA ROMAGNA AND THE MARCHES
(Emilia Romagna and Marche)

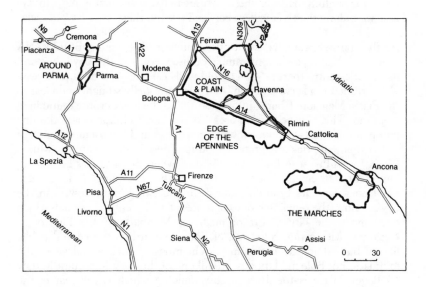

Although this region abounds with fascinating and often famous cities, it is not well known to visitors who still tend to follow the Venice – Florence – Rome axis. It's true that scenically it is perhaps less appealing to some tastes than other regions, for much of Emilia Romagna is flat and heavily cultivated, and the area of the Marches has no one drawing card to identify it touristically. Nevertheless, the visitor will find much to enjoy in this stretch of Adriatic coastline, often completely uncrowded and seeming to appeal only to local people. To sit in a café in Bologna is to sample life as Italians know it, and with a few words of Italian to be treated as an honoured guest rather than part of a vast and shifting crowd suffered by waiters, taxi drivers and hotel receptionists as necessary for income, as can happen in some of the famous centres. Bologna is a particularly fascinating city with a vital life and a reputation as one of the greatest gastronomical centres of Italy. It is also replete with fine shops and an array of architectural treasures — which can often be viewed from

51

the shelter of an arcade, for the city has miles of covered pavements — from every period it seems. 'Industrial centre' hardly sums up Bologna — although there *are* many factories and the autostrade hum with trucks and vans — for within the circle of the old walls is an island of calm and order, busy and yet not too frenetic to neglect Italian politeness and warmth.

Bologna is an ideal centre to stop in, for there is a large range of hotels (ours was the Jolly, part of a chain, but well run and very comfortable, close to the railway station which is a major junction for those coming by rail, or using a rail-car connection). You could also base yourself in Ferrara, or Ravenna, or, in the Marches, Urbino — although here the centre is Ancona for those who like the sea and the life of a port. Roads in Emilia Romagna are good and in the valley of the Po very straight and level: in the hilly parts of these two areas roads inevitably tend to run east-west along the river valleys between the hill ridges.

As the starting point for two of the routes in this region, **BOLOGNA** (pop: 495,000) repays a long ramble of discovery, and this city is larger in its historic centre than most. The old walls can still be traced, otherwise wide arcaded roads cut through the town, unusually straight and clear to the Piazza Maggiore (tourist information) and the great bronze fountain of Neptune. This is a pedestrian area, so you can well appreciate the fine group of buildings — the town hall, the palaces and the sombre church of S. Petronio, all brick and grandly Gothic. There is a museum (the Museo Civico) with Etruscan finds from the days when Bologna was Felsina, an important settlement. Be sure to see the charming little Palazzo Bevilacqua with its beautiful courtyard; the two leaning towers in the city's centre (the remaining ones of scores of 12th-century originals which once made the city a sort of medieval Manhattan); the Pinacotèca Nazionale with a fine collection of Bolognese artists; the central public library housed in the handsome Archiginnasio, once a college in the foundation of Bologna University (still one of the most important in Italy — Poggi Palace is the 16th-century building which is the seat of the university at Porta S. Donata); the Isolani house at Strada Maggiore where an arcade was first constructed to lean against the façade of the palace thereby creating more room — and a new style (there are 35km of arcades or porticoes in the city); the much altered duòmo and many other churches, but most notably the cluster of ancient edifices from the Romanesque period known as Santo Stefano. There are many other museums in addition to the ones mentioned — from industrial art to one displaying toy soldiers. The memorial to the dead of two wars is in the Piazza del Nettuno, and there is a striking glass tablet inscribed with the names of those who died in the terrible Bologna railway station explosion (but even more impressive is the memorial in the station itself — a giant crack in the second-class waiting room has been glazed and left mutely to indicate the terrible tragedy). Close by is the bus station and a handsome park, reached up a flight of steps, and with a view of one of the city gates, marooned now in the midst of traffic. There is enough to see on several walks, and the medieval streets of Bologna are particularly interesting.

Plan to eat well here — it may not be cheap, but it *will* be
worthwhile. **Le Tre Frecce** is charming in atmosphere with an air of
old-style elegance (051-231200) and **Il Battibecco** (051-275845) comes
well recommended as does the **Motel Agip** (051-401130) which is
reasonable and yet keeps up the standards in this great city of Italian
gastronomy. Bologna hotels: **Jolly**, Piazza XX Settembre (051-264405);
Europa, Via G Bolfrini, 4 (051-232461).

Coast and Plain

1 day or longer/250km/from Bologna

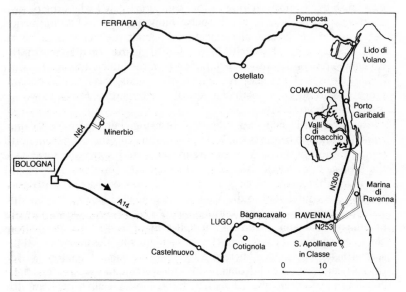

Italy is now so well supplied with autostrade it is almost difficult to leave a
major city without using one, and Bologna is such a major centre.
However, if you persevere you will be able to navigate to lesser known
roads, but sometimes it is as well to use a major road for the first few
kilometres of a journey to get out of the city. For this particular route it
would be better to follow the green signs for A14 and Ravenna. You will
find yourself on the outer ring of autostrade around the city heading on
an extension of this trunk road to the east. About 7km from the city
centre it leaves the ganglia of support roads and arrows towards Ravenna,
changing towards that city at Castelnuovo. At Cotignola leave the main
road at the interchange.

COTIGNOLA is a small village, famous for being the birthplace of
the ducal family of the Sforza in the 14th century. It has an interesting
church. Follow signs for **LUGO** where there is an arcaded market of the
18th century and a medieval castle keep, both well preserved despite the

heavy fighting suffered in World War II. (If you preferred to take a longer non-motorway route to Lugo on 253 from Bologna you rejoin the main route here.) Through vineyards you follow directions for **BAGNACAVALLO**, where there is a very early church, S. Pietro in Silva, with fine frescoes of the 14th century. In the nunnery here, Allegra, the infant daughter of Byron, died. Continue towards Ravenna on 253 across flat land paralleling the autostrada part of the way.

RAVENNA is one of the most extraordinary of towns with its great number of Byzantine buildings and churches. The modern city is dull, and surrounded by large petrochemical refineries and industrial suburbs, but the interest for the visitor is all contained well within the old city. Once a shipyard but now far from the sea, the city could claim space for 250 Roman ships. Its most exciting history came in AD 402 when the Roman court was moved here by the Emperor Honorius and a glittering period began under his sister Galla Placidia who built the main monuments. With the invasion of the city in the fourth quarter of the century the Roman empire of the west ended, but early in the 6th century it was taken by Belisarius and the Eastern Emperor, Justinian; his wife, Theodora, proceeded to adorn it so that much of the Byzantine Ravenna we see today dates from this time.

Ravenna easily takes up a day's sightseeing, but it is easy walking, being flat and the centre is small. The Via Roma cuts the town from north to south. Most of the monuments are in the western sector. Be sure to see the Basilica of S. Vitale, with its magnificent array of mosaics of the 6th century. It has a circular campanile, a style common here. A path leads through the churchyard to the Mausoleum of Galla Placidia. It is a small, unprepossessing building containing fine mosaics in dark blue with figures of humans and animals and a constellation of stars, all dimly lit from alabaster windows. (Take small change to illuminate the mosaics with the special lights provided.) There are two baptistery buildings (one beside the cathedral was once a Roman bath and has fine mosaics on its double arcadings; the other, also octagonal, has a mosaic ceiling depicting the twelve apostles) and a further splendid church, S. Apollinare Nuovo. There are two strips of mosaic in this church running along the nave and depicting biblical scenes, but most interesting are the ones relating to Ravenna itself with views of its principal buildings and a procession of martyrs, and the opposite mosaic has views of the ancient port of Classis and a procession of virgin martyrs and the magi. There are 24 marble columns (antique from Greece) and a handsome flat panelled ceiling. San Francesco also has antique columns and a 10th-century campanile. There are several sites with Roman remains and next to 15th-century cloisters the tomb of Dante (18th century) covering the 15th-century tomb and, in turn, the older sarcophagus. Each year the city of Florence supplies fresh oil for the votive lamp. There is a small museum. The city also has a museum of antiquities housed in two charming cloisters near S. Vitale, and a picture gallery, the Belle Arti, with Bellini and Vivarini works as well as Longhi and Paris Bordone. A recommended restaurant in the town (moderately expensive) is **Tre Spade** (0544-32382).

In the environs of Ravenna are the beach resort known as **MARINA DI RAVENNA** beside the opening of the Candiano canal and with a good sand beach; and the great and impressive architectural grouping of the basilica of S. Apollinare in Classe, near the Classe pinewood. Here, at the site of the Roman port of Classis just south of modern Rimini, is this church of great distinction with mosaics and Greek columns with Byzantine bases and Corinthinian capitals. Follow the main 309 back into the city and continue north, or a farther detour may be made following the left bank of the inlet just after the turn off of 61 for Marina di Ravenna, and exploring the lagoons along the coast via Marina Romea.

This is mysterious country, swampy and mist draped, the fine nets used to catch the eels (local delicacies) giving a theatrical effect to the inlets and marshy banks. Pass through the Pineta S. Vitale on 309 and look for signs for the little hut where Garibaldi hid in 1849, actually a reconstruction of the patriot's hideout. The road continues on to pass **COMACCHIO** (pop: 21,000) where eel fishing is the major industry and vast numbers are caught and cured in the autumn migration to the sea. The town is very curious, with an odd, unsettling atmosphere, due partly no doubt to its situation, but it can hardly be described as friendly and the inhabitants look on visitors to their isolated town with suspicion. Park and walk along the canals to look at the handsome Palazzo Bellini on the canal, having walked over the odd three-way bridge that provides entrance to the town, the 17th-century Trepponti. To the north-west is an ancient Etruscan necropolis, recently excavated at the remains of the port of **SPINA**. The many objects from the town's 4th century BC heyday are now at Ferrara. Continue on 309 leaving behind the vast Valli di Comacchio, a wide and much drained lagoon once a bird sanctuary for waders and gulls, as you head towards the great swampy delta of the Po, and standing like an exclamation mark on the horizon, the belltower of the Abbey of Pomposa. The suggested route is off on a minor coast road to Lido de Volano, passing through wide fields of rice, then turning left for **POMPOSA**, but you may drive directly there on 309.

The abbey is both ancient and famous, for here Guido d'Arezzo, a monk, first invented the modern musical scale. There are fine pavement mosaics in the big church with its frescoes (dating from the 9th century), with later enlargements. The Benedictines, who founded the abbey in the 7th century, attempted drainage schemes for the marshes which had to be abandoned, as did the monastery, eventually, when the Po altered its channel and malarial infestations began. The church and its buildings are now owned by the government and open to the public — note in particular the unusual *palazzo della ragione*, the court of justice, 11th-century and arcaded. The tall campanile is decorated with small gleaming plaques and the fine windows increase towards its lofty pointed roof. Pomposa is very popular with visitors and a whole area of stalls springs up on weekends — try to go during the week when it is quieter and less noisy.

Drive along the road towards Codigoro along the valley of the little Po di Volano, with a stop perhaps at **OSTELLATO** where there is ruined castle, looking over the now-drained Lake of Comacchio. The road continues through unprepossessing scenery paralleling the railway and near the motorway to arrive at one of the most fascinating towns in Italy, the home of the great dukes of Este, **FERRARA** (pop: 165,000).

Not far from the wide Po, this small and vibrant little city has regained much of its prosperity from new industry and increased agricultural activity in the region. Ferrara was once one of Italy's most important cities, and its industry attracted the bombing raids of World War II. It has a well-defined centre and the city walls have been turned to gardens and a promenade. In the 15th century the enlightened first duke, Ercole, laid out new sections of the city; the next duke, Alfonso, was married to Lucrezia Borgia, and the poet Ariosto, whose house can be seen, was Alfonso's friend — continuing a long tradition among the Este family of encouraging the arts; although under the following duke Ercole, life was much less glittering at the courts since his wife, Renée, daughter of the king of France, became a Calvinist. Her chapel can be seen in the great brick castle sitting solidly in the centre of the city. Calvin himself visited his famous convert here. Her son, Alsonso II, was the patron of Tasso, who lived in the town. Earlier artists patronised by the Estes include Pisanello, Cosmé Tura and Dosso Dossi, and the town was the birthplace of Frescobaldi, the composer, Rossetti, the architect and Savonarola, the religious reformer.

Aside from the castle, which can be visited, although it is almost devoid of furnishings and some rooms are used for exhibitions — descend to the gloomy dungeons under the waterline of the moat — the principal buildings are the cathedral, the *palazzo del comune*, the great stairway in the Piazza Municipio, the clocktower, the Pinacotèca with paintings of the Ferrarese School and many palaces. Try to see the palace of Ludovico il Moro (Etruscan and Greek articles from Spina); the Palazzo dei Diamanti (Diamonds), from the cut of the stones on the façade, the emblem of the Este family; and in particular the Schifanoia, known to the Estes as their palace of pleasures. In the south-east of the town be sure to walk along the medieval streets off the Via delle Volte, the most picturesque of Ferrara's streets. Try **Trattoria da Ido** for a meal in Ferrarese style (0532-421064) or for a snack and local pastries both sweet and savoury the **Leon d'Oro** on the Piazza Municipio. From Ferrara route 64 will return you direct to Bologna, stopping perhaps at **MINERBIO** where there is a castle with a very tall six-sided tower. You also have the choice of the A13 autostrada back.

Edge of the Apennines

One day/240km/from Bologna

From Bologna the road goes, straight and direct, to Imola. Route 9 passes in the shade of the mountains to the right and is indeed the old Via Emilia. It passes through **CASTEL S. PIETRO** with the remains of a

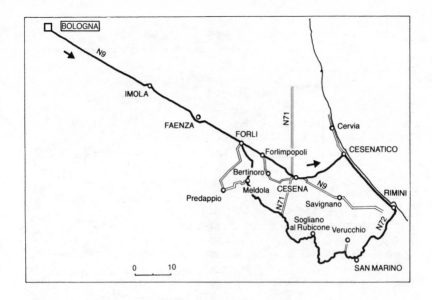

13th-century castle, also a spa with mud baths fed by sulphurous springs. A little farther along, a delightful detour can be made to the right to the little village of **DOZZA**, which is an artists' retreat and has gaily painted walls — the main street is an open-air gallery. The town is situated on a hill around its Rocca, which may be visited and where you can purchase the local wine in cool cellars — the champagne-like one is very good and cheap, if a little sweet, but it makes an elegant dessert wine. After about 33km you will reach **IMOLA** (pop: 63,000) with a picture gallery in a former convent, and the palace of the Volpe. The duòmo is entirely 18th-century work, and so is the *palazzo comunale*. The castle with a large round tower is 14th century and here the daughter of a Sforza, Caterina Riario, faced Cesare Borgia's army in 1500.

The road goes right through the town, but you may skirt it to the north if you wish and continue on towards Faenza. Before this town is **CASTEL BOLOGNESE**, with remnants of a fortress also subdued by the Borgia son. To the south is a small spa town, popular in summer, **RIOLO TERME**, with a fortress.

FAENZA (pop: 60,000) gave its name to the pottery known as 'faïence' and some is still made here, and is on sale in souvenir shops. Each year potters compete in a competition held here. Not surprisingly there is a museum of ceramics of all parts of Italy, with a modern section featuring works from many countries, There is also a school of ceramics. The duòmo is 15th century with an unfinished façade and a handsome, three-aisled interior in the Tuscan manner. The Piazza del Popolo has a lively market on Thursdays, which is perhaps not the best day to see the arcaded square with its 17th-century clocktower and two medieval

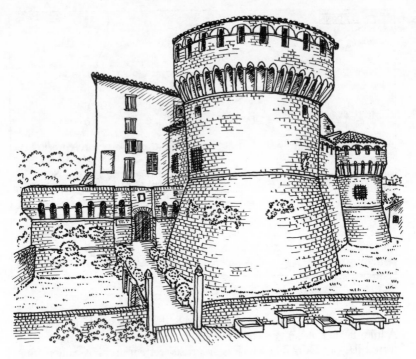

Rocca di Dozza

palaces. There is also an art gallery with pictures and sculptures. Two interesting churches of the town are the Commenda (Romanesque) and Santa Maria Vecchia with an early campanile. The town was badly damaged in World War II.

The road goes on to Forli, where the road dips to the right if you wish to drive on without entering the town. **FORLÌ** (pop: 115,000) is the most important town of the area, the Romagna. The central square, Piazza Saffi, named after a native, Aurelio Saffi, an architect of Italian liberty in the 19th century, contains a large church, that of S. Mercuriale. The tall campanile is of the 12th century, as is the foundation of the church though it was altered later, being transformed in the 18th century. The cloister, reopened as a public walkway, is very handsome. Nearby is the 15th-century municipal palace, a neighbour to the 19th-century cathedral off the Corso Garibaldi. The campanile was once a tower of a family house owned by the Orgogliosi; they rivalled the Ordelaffi who gave their name to this piazza. There is a castle, now a prison, once besieged by Cesare Borgia, and a picture gallery with examples of Fra Angelico, Guercino and Lorenzo di Credi. A reasonably priced restaurant, with local wines, is in the **Principe** (0543-29362) — original dishes.

Drive on towards Ronco and the direction of Cesena, passing through (on route 9) the village of **FORLIMPOPOLI**, with a castle of the Ordelaffi, now containing a museum and theatre — there is a festival here in March. Not far off is **BERTINORO**, a hill town with walls, surrounded by vineyards, for the town is famous for its wines and its pastries — there is a fine view from the piazza, which contains a 14th-century palazzo municipale and a curious column with rings for horses. The castle became a hotel: it has had a violent warlike history. Continue on to Cesena.

At **CESENA** (pop: 95,000) the road crosses the N71 before entering the town, which is sited on the banks of the Savio, overshadowed by a hill on which, above the trees, stands the 15th-century Rocca Malatestiana. Each August trotting championships are held at the racecourse, drawing great crowds. The town exports fruit and preserves. Its most interesting building (and the one to see if you don't wish to dally) is the Biblioteca Malatestiana, named after the 14th-century ruling family. This fine library, open every morning till 1 pm, contains manuscripts with miniatures — its main gallery is 40m long and is a handsome three-aisled room with white columns of marble.

Just outside Cesena is a British military cemetery on the road to Cervia. From 9 just beyond the centre of Cesena a road, 304, takes you across the plain to the fascinating port of **CESENATICO**, on the Adriatic, with a harbour designed by Leonardo da Vinci. This alone would be enough to make it a 'must-see', but in addition Cesenatico is a bathing place and a museum of ships — the little harbour is filled with a variety of examples of local craft, a brilliant sight. Excellent restaurants and hotels can be found here, with many of course serving fish and seafood — try the simple and reasonable **Punta Nord** (0547-81446) for lunch on a sunny terrace, or for fish alone try **Gallo di Giorgio** (0547-81067), moderately expensive. Just north of Cesenatico, along the coast you come to the busy port of **CERVIA**, where each year the marriage of the sea is celebrated on Ascension Day, with the local bishop throwing a ring into the sea. The town is old (17th century) and walled, but surrounded by an extensive resort among its widespread pinewoods, which scent the sea air.

Return along the coast road, through Cesenatico, passing a long string of continuous resorts known as the Riviera di Rimini, fine beaches and summer hotels, crowded in summer as is **RIMINI** (pop: 130,000) itself, the most popular resort on the Adriatic, with many British and German tourists. The resort clustered along an extensive promenade, the Lungomare Vittorio Emanuele, has kilometres of beach and excellent sea bathing. Parallel to the Lungomare is the Viale Amerigo Vespucci, which has shops and cafés, always open late during the summer season. The resort is separated from the town by the rail line, and old Rimini is well worth a visit. The town was much damaged in 1944, but the buildings, particularly the Tempio Malatestiano, a remarkable Renaissance monument, part church, part depiction of temporal power, have been well restored. The tempio, now the cathedral of Rimini, is worth an

Cesenatico harbour

extended visit, but you should also see the Ponte Augusto, a Roman bridge across the Marecchia river; the Arch of Augustus (27BC marking the point at which two great Roman roads, the Via Flaminia and the Via Emilia converge); several medieval buildings and the early church of S. Agostino with 14th-century frescoes. In the Palazzo del Podesta is a fine collection of ethnological art from Africa and Oceania. A friendly restaurant is **Dallo Zio** (0541-52325) with fish specialities.

Undoubtedly the most popular excursion for people visiting Rimini is up the hill to the little republic of **SAN MARINO** (pop: 20,000). Follow N72 out of the town and across the plain until you arrive at the frontier — there are no formalities but you may obtain a stamp in your passport if you wish, usually for a fee. The capital is tiny and charming with narrow streets (no cars allowed) and shops sell souvenirs — ceramics and postage stamps are popular (Italian currency is used). There is an art gallery (pictures by Guercino and Ribera; Egyptian, Roman and Etruscan antiquities) and three citadels from which you may obtain fine views to the sea, but you do not need to climb to the heights of Monte Titano for these since the main square and numerous terraces also give panoramic views. Leave the town and turn left along a winding road descending through Acquaviva to the border of San Marino and the junction with 258, where a left turn is made towards Villanova. (You can backtrack a short distance along the valley of the Marecchia to see a hill-town, **VERRUCHIO**, with a Malatesta castle on the Scorticato hill — this was the birthplace of the family.) Cross the river and leave the briefly entered region of the Marche towards **SOGLIANO AL RUBICONE**, on the river Rubicone (Caesar's Rubicon) along narrow picturesque hill roads.

Take the left turn and follow the road via Montegelli to its intersection with N71 — turn right and follow this road for about 6km to Borello, where you turn left across the foothills of the Apennines towards **MELDOLA** with its castle. Here you can make a detour to see **PREDAPPIO**, the birthplace of Benito Mussolini, who had several of the town's public buildings erected and who is buried in the cemetery. You can rejoin the route at Forli by following 9 ter from here. From Meldola follow 310 down to Forli and return to Bologna the way you came (or alternatively take the A14 autostrada from Forli).

Around Parma
1 day/100km/from Parma

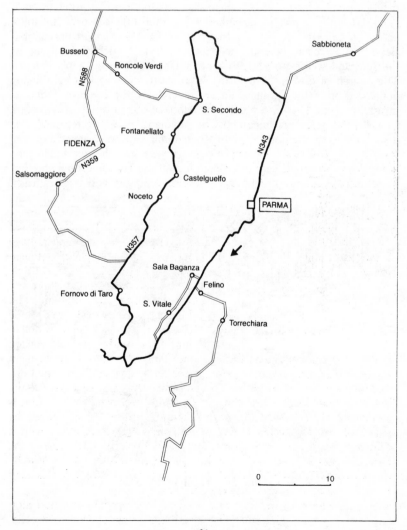

Using Parma as a base you can follow a neat circular route into the surrounding country, both hill and plain, to see and sample some of the area's famous products — notably Parma ham and Parmesan cheese. It is more than just an educative trip, for you will find the local farmers proud of their products and genuinely happy to show you the methods of preparation.

PARMA (pop: 185,000) makes a useful and attractive base and is a city with much to offer the walker, having a particularly fine assemblage of ancient buildings and good hotels and restaurants. Note particularly the beautiful baptistery, long closed for restoration of its red marbles, is frieze and the remarkable frescoes of its eight-sided interior. Like the neighbouring cathedral it is Romanesque, giving the Piazza del Duòmo great style and harmony. The cathedral has a tall 13th-century campanile and its interior is decorated with works of Corregio and sculptures by Benedetto Antelami (also in the Baptistery) and Bianchini. Opposite is the fine and well-restored 13th-century façade of the Bishop's Palace. The church of S. Giovanni Evangelista has frescoes by Corregio in its dome and others by Parmigianino in the chapels; the medieval *farmacia* nearby has kept its 16th-century decorations of carved wood and frescoes as well as its ancient equipment. The huge and rather decrepit Palazzo della Pilotta was the home of the Farnese family and was damaged in the war; it contains the spectacular Farnese Theatre (rebuilt after 1944) and the Galleria Nazionale with many paintings of the Emilian school and the Museum of Antiquities, containing pottery, sculpture and bronzes from

Farnese Theatre, Parma

the Roman town of Velleia. Parma had many rulers, then the Farnese took over in the mid-16th century, holding it through the Bourbon-Parma family until the early 19th century, when it was ceded to the Empress of Napoleon, Marie-Louise — her second husband, Neipperg, is buried in the church of the Madonna della Steccata, a Bramante-inspired building. Marie-Louise also had built the large Teatro Regio at which a youthful Toscanini, born in Parma, played in the orchestra. Paganini is buried here; born in the area, Verdi started work here, and Stendhal set *The Charterhouse of Parma* here. The local Jolly hotel is called the **Jolly Stendhal**, others are the **Bristol** and the **Principe**. A recommended restaurant in this gastronomic centre is **Parizzi**, moderately expensive (0521-25952) — a better bargain is **Al Tribunale** (0521-25527) a welcoming old family restaurant.

From Parma follow roads south to the outskirts of the city and then turn right along a country road towards Sala Baganza on the valley of the Baganza river. This valley is virtually down the middle of the Parma ham country, and there are signs to indicate visits to farms. (If you are nervous about 'dropping in' check with the information office in Parma as to which places offer welcome, and where English may be spoken.) At Sala Baganza you may make a detour south along the river to a ham factory — or *prosciuttificio*, I visited not long ago. The modern Prosciuttificio S. Giacomo at S. Vitale stands in the lee of low wooded hills and you are shown the complete process — allow at least an hour and take something warm, the cold-storage can be really chilly (for enquiries 0521-830179). The main route along the east bank passes **FELINO** with its castle and continues on to Calestano through typical scenery, gently wooded and attractive especially if your visit is in the autumn or early spring.

Over to the left on the *torrente* Parma is **TORRECHIARA**, a town on a hill with a castle built by the Sforzas — it contains the Golden Room, decorated by Bembo in tiles and frescoes. Close by are ski resorts in the mountains, especially at **SCHIA**, on Monte Caio to the south. Descend from Calestano to **FORNOVO DI TARO** where you will find in this village a fine church, with sculptures on the façade by pupils of Antelami. Cross the Taro here and continue noth on 357 towards Noceto. [A detour can be made to the left to see the birthplace of the composer Verdi at Roncole, visiting also the towns of **SALSOMAGGIORE** with its extensive thermal establishments (there are several spas in the area) and **FIDENZA** on 359 in the valley of the Stirone, the river marking the western limit of the Parma ham region. The duòmo has a fine doorway with flanking statues from Antelami's pupils, and the tomb of S. Donnino, a Roman-Christian soldier who was martyred here. Drive north on 588 towards **BUSSETO** where there is a small Verdi museum and an assembly of charming buildings decorated with terracotta ornamentation, as well as a 16th-century castle with battlements and a Gothic town hall. Just north of the town is **VILLA DI S. AGATE**, a country house built by the composer and open to view — relics on show. Take the road towards S. Secondo to rejoin the main route passing through **RONCOLE**

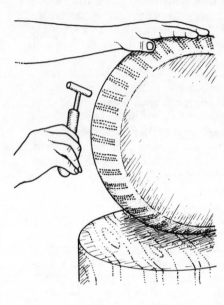

Parmesan cheese

VERDI, where the composer's birthplace may be seen. At SORAGNA there is an art gallery in the castle.]

The main route continues up the valley of the Taro beside the autostrade; a parallel country road to the left can also be taken to NOCETO. Here there is a castle and an attractive fortress, also another at CASTELGUELFO called once the Torre d'Orlando. Cross N9 and at FONTANEL-LATO look for the handsome 13th-century castle with its moat (open all year, closed Mon); Parmigianino decorations. At SAN SECONDO there is a castle of the Rossis, with frescoes. Throughout this area you will find farms producing Parmesan cheese — enquire at 8B Via Marco dell'Arpa in Parma where you may watch the process, which is most interesting. Continue to ROCCABIANCA where there is a Rossi castle beside the Po. Cross the meandering Taro and head for COLORNO where there is a palace of the Farnese family. A detour north across the long bridge over the Po will take you to SABBIONETA, a town of the Gonzaga family, well-laid out and with many monuments. Town walls enclose 'little Athens' as it was known under the Vespasian Gonzaga. There is a fine Teatro Olimpico and ducal palace. Return to Parma by the direct N343.

The Marches
1 day/250km/from Ancona

The hilly region of the Marches stretches between the Abruzzo and adjoins Emilia Romagna, taking up a large piece of the 'calf' of the Italian boot. There is a fine coastline with sandy beaches and excellent swimming and sunbathing at the many little Adriatic resorts, which are connected with a railway line going from Pesaro in the north to Porto d'Ascoli in the south, passing the capital of the region, Ancona, half-way along on its spur of land. The autostrada A14 also parallels this route.

Inland the Marches are composed of green hills and river valleys, running down the eastern slope of the Apennine chain in a north-easterly direction to the sea. This is an area that is almost entirely agricultural and, under Roman domination, when the local people, the Piceni, had been

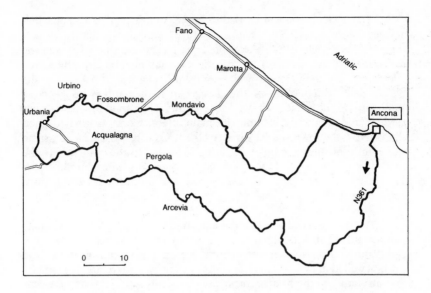

subdued after many insurrections, the Marches were the Imperial food basket with agricultural produce and grain providing Rome with a prime source of food. The coastal strip has exotic vegetation and is densely populated and flat until the rise of the hills which become steeper and rougher as you penetrate south-west towards the mountains.

The capital, **ANCONA** (pop. of area 115,000) has a theatrical setting above the sea and is an important port and ferry terminal to international destinations. There is an airport, and rail connections. An earthquake in 1972 destroyed many of the old houses in the part spread across Monte Guasco, and much is being restored, but still the old town repays a long ramble if you choose Ancona as your base for this route. A growing place, Ancona has spreading suburbs and a wide 19th-century planned town with avenues and squares. Like most of the ports of the Adriatic, Ancona suffered from bombing in the latter part of World War II, also from the fire of the Austrian fleet in World War I. As a result there is little old left in the port area and people have moved out of the centre, but the harbour is busy and the new sections of the city seem well planned and prosperous. There is a modern art gallery in the Palazzo Bosdari; also on the Via Pizzecoli as it climbs up the hill is the Palazzo Ferretti where there is a museum of the Marches. Right on the top of the mountain that overlooks the harbour is the cathedral, St Cyriacus — it has been badly damaged in this century yet still keeps much of its original Romanesque work with a 14th-century campanile. Unusual architectural features are the 12-sided cupola and ancient columns from the Roman temples originally occupying the mountain top. There is a museum and a bishop's palace and from the square wide views. Another fine church is S. Maria della Piazza, which you will be glad to know doesn't require a steep climb as does the duòmo! There is a 13th-century façade and sculptures. Other things to see include the Arch of Trajan (2nd century AD) on the harbourside, and a later 18th-century triumphal arch, the Arco Clementino — they are also well seen from the cathedral piazza. On the Piazza della Repubblica is the Loggia dei Mercanti with a good Venetian-Gothic façade of the 15th century. The modern quarter has gardens and shaded walks and the main street, Corso Garibaldi, good shops. Near the town the **RIVIERA DEL CONERO** has beaches, some stony, and this hilly road gives pleasing sea views to the point where the road diverges for **PORTONOVA** where there is a fine church of the 10th century, a gem of Romanesque work and untouched it seems since construction.

From Ancona proceed towards the autostrada and N361 which will take you towards **OSIMO**, which was the main city of the Piceni. There is a cathedral with a baptistery containing a bronze 17th-century font. The town is walled and as a reminder of its ancient past there are decapitated Roman statues in the *palazzo comunale* (16th century). The road here goes towards Macerata with wide views but a side trip may be made to the famous religious centre of **LORETO** along a narrow road towards the sea — this is one of Italy's best known places of pilgrimage to see the supposed birthplace of Mary the Virgin. The house was carried here by divine agents in 1291, the devout believe! It is now covered by a suitably grandiose church which contains many treasures. Loreto itself is charming with 16th-century town walls and battlements and a handsome arcaded piazza, plus a museum containing tapestries and majolica.

Return to the route by backtracking through **CASTELFIDARDO** with its ossuary and a battle-site of 1860, or through the town of **RECANATI** where Gigli was born (there is a museum to the tenor's memory). The house of the poet Leopardi can be visited in summer and the central piazza with its monument to the poet contains the impressive 13th century Torre del Borgo. The route can be rejoined at **MONTEFANO** where the local wine can be sampled. South is **MONTECASSIANO** with a fine church and ancient fortifications and **MACERATA** with fine views and a chapel which in 1772 witnessed the wedding of Prince Charles Stuart. Continue along a valley towards Arpignano then turn right on another back road towards **CINGOLI**. This little town has spectacular views over the hills, nicknamed the 'balcony of the Marche', for you can see as far as the Adriatic from the belvedere beyond S. Francesco. 502 goes north for about 10km before turning right towards Staffolo and on to Cupromontana where there are thermal establishments. Follow the road on to turn left onto N76, then right after 6km towards **ARCEVIA**, a local craft centre with two Signorelli works in the church of S. Menardo. Turn left on N360 for a very short distance then right on a road across the hills to **PERGOLA**, where there is a rail terminus from Fabriano coming through **SASSOFERRATO**, the home of the painter of 17th-century madonnas.

In the town museum are finds from the Roman settlement of Sentinum and mosaics.

From Pergola take N424 towards **CAGLI** which has a fine *palazzo comunale* and a Rocca with a big tower. Turn right towards Acqualagna in the direction of Urbino. Instead of following the route into the mountains you can if you wish make a short-cut from here across the hills towards Urbino via Fermignano (Bramante was born here). The route, however, makes a detour to the west to **PIOBBICO**, a mountain health centre for skiing and also for exploring caves. If you wish you may continue on 257 up the valley towards Citta di Castello and eventually Rome. Our route turns right across the hilltops to **URBANIA** named after a pope (Urban VIII) and a centre for the pottery known as majolica, which can be purchased here. There are some interesting medieval buildings and a collection of drawings at the Ducal Palace. The main road continues along up the Metaura valley towards Arezzo, but our route crosses the river and ascends the hills in the direction of Urbino, with good views of the town in the distance, some 20km away.

URBINO (pop: 18,000) is a fascinating survival and would amply repay a day's stopover. Huge walls enclose the little city Raphael, Bramante and other artists knew well under the patronage of an enlightened ducal family, notably Federico da Montefeltro. The town dates from pre-Roman times, but it became notable when the Montefeltro family came into power in the 12th century, reaching its apogee as a centre of culture under Federico and later under his son and the ensuing duke, Francesco Maria della Rovere — both he and Federico received the Order of the Garter from English monarchs. The city had a narrow escape from destruction in 1944.

Steep and narrow streets, some stepped, rise up to the principal buildings, of which the main one is the great limestone palace of Laurana's design — the ducal palace is without a doubt one of the most magnificent in Italy, a great monument of the Renaissance. The Court of Honour has semi-circular arches and a grand stair; the façade has loggias and two high towers with decorations by Barocci. The upper storey contains the pictures of the National Gallery of the Marches. The duke's study, all inlay work, is justly famous; the little chapel and the temple of the Muses should be seen and there is a fine view from the loggia in the north-west tower. The Throne Room contains tapestries from the Gobelins and the Room of the Angels is named after the dancing *putti* on the great fireplace. The palace rings with famous names — Botticelli, Verocchio, Uccello, della Francesca and, of course, Raphael, who was born here. The house of the painter is on the Via Raffaello, which may be visited. There are several fine churches and the duòmo is in good contrast, being neo-classical, reconstructed after an earthquake of 200 years ago. There is a museum. You can also go on an extended walk to see the Fortezza, which can be visited, and the arched Corso Garibaldi with a good view of the palace. There are small hotels within the city walls and a very reasonable restaurant is **Il Nuovo Coppiere** (0722-41350) in the centre of the town with home-made pasta.

From Urbino take the road down the valley towards **FOSSOMBRONE**, with Roman ruins. (Note just outside Urbino the church of S. Bernardo with the impressive tombs of the Dukes in black marble and a terrace with a good view.) Fossombrone itself has a bishop's palace and museum. Take the minor road towards Sant'Ippolito, or a detour may be made along the valley of the Metauro to **FANO** on the coast where there is a good beach and Roman walls as well as a triumphal arch of the 2nd century AD. The route continues across country to **MONDAVIO** with a formidable fortress of the 15th century. Bear left on 424 towards **MAROTTA**, a resort on the coast, and almost immediately turn to the right to **CORINALDO**. Here you find a town with 15th-century walls, and good campsites. Continue on towards Ostra Vetere and cross the N360 bearing right and taking the next turn on the left towards Jesi. (N360 for **SENIGALLIA**, with its castle and arcaded Via Portici Ercolani, and hotels on the sea.)

JESI (or Iesi) was the birthplace of Pergolesi. It has a palace by Martini and Sansovino with a gallery containing Roman works and paintings by Lotto and Guercino. The town has 14th-century walls. From here follow the road (along the valley of the Esino) down towards the sea, passing the airport on the right and then taking a short stretch of coast road back to Ancona. Hotels here include the **Roma e Pace** with recommended restaurant (071-55612). **Passeto** (071-33214) is a highly rated restaurant, but dear.

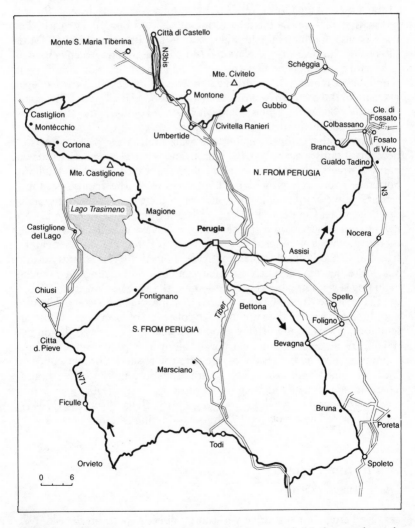

'Italy has a green heart — Umbria', it has been said. Umbria is the only region of Italy that is totally landlocked and Perugia is at the very centre of the 'green heart', a splendid city massed along the top of a hill, as are so many towns and villages here. Wide sweeping views of the valley of the Tiber are obtained as you climb the steep height of the solitary hill and enter the town.

PERUGIA (pop: 105,000) has an ancient history and Etruscan origins — walks should include a visit to the Porta Marzia and the Arch of Augustus, both from that period when Perugia was known as Aperusia. There are also many fine medieval houses and the fountain before the duòmo (which has been long in restoration, swathed in scaffolding) is one of the most striking Gothic ones in the country — it dates from 1298 and has many sculptures by the famous master, Nicolo Pisano. The cathedral itself is also Gothic, rare in Italy, and it has its own museum. Most interesting, however, is the National Museum of Umbria which is housed in several handsome and plain rooms of the Palazzo dei Priori nearby — it is open all year and well worth an extended visit. Next to it is the Collegio el Cambio, the old 15th-century exchange, also open all year. It has some surprising woodwork, panels inlaid with detailed designs, and also a series of fine frescoes by Perugino and his pupils.

If the weather is fine, pursue your walk around the town — it is of necessity tightly packed on its hilltop and offers sudden views down narrow streets — one is so odd as to be called the Via Bagliona Sotteranea, or underground road. Not far off is the handsome 15th-century university building, and also near to it on Piazza Matteotti is the Palazzo del Capitano del Popolo, dating from 1472. At the end of a neighbouring loggia you can look over a wide view of valley and hill. But then, panoramas are offered in several sites in Perugia — another can be found at Piazzo Raffaello, after you have climbed the fine stairway of the Via Volte della Pace. There are many fascinating buildings in Perugia, including several notable churches — one, the vast S. Domenico, is also the home of the Museo Civico, housed in a one-time monastery. The first floor houses a large and comprehensive collection of Roman and Etruscan sculpture, jewellery and artefacts (open all year and holidays). If you are staying in Perugia take time to walk along the pedestrianised Corso Vannucci where all the residents seem to stroll at sunset, or take coffee or chocolate piled with *panna* at the atmospheric Sandri's coffee house. There are many small tempting shops, most open until 7.30.

An excellent old-style hotel in Perugia is the **Bella Vista** (075-27041), centrally placed in the city and with rooms offering panoramic views.

South from Perugia

1 day or longer/185km

Leaving Perugia for this drive you can go directly south on the old 397, crossing the country to arrive at Bevagna or, for a fast route, take the main 75 south to Foligno and then right through Maceratola, after

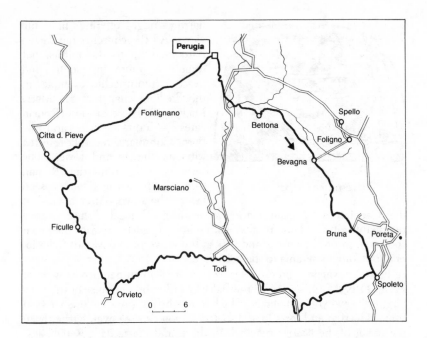

exploring **FOLIGNO** (pop: 50,000). This busy, well-placed town has a cathedral with a fine Romanesque door with important sculptures and a delicate loggia. The interior is an 18th-century transformation scene. An arcade joins the duòmo to the Palazzo Trinci, which contains the town museum. There are pleasant walks within the old town, which is girdled by a circular avenue. After quitting the town via the Porta Todi follow the road to Bevagna. If you elect to follow the 397 from Perugia, which is more scenic, turn off it at St Martino (left) and proceed to **TORGIANO** where you cross the Chiascio river before it tumbles into the Tiber. Follow the road on about 5km to **BETTONA**. Here you will discover a most picturesque town on a hill with splendid views over the river. There are Etruscan remains here: the walls are partly 4th century BC, and near the little town (which also proudly parades its own art gallery in the Palazzo dei Podesta, a handsome building of the 14th century) are Etruscan burial grounds.

Descend from Bettona towards Passagio and follow the road along the river valley to **BEVAGNA**. This small town has a charming piazza and two noteworthy churches. First to S. Sylvestre with a plain Romanesque interior, and a raised choir with the crypt beneath — a very satisfying little place. S. Michele is slightly later and has a splendid doorway framed with a parade of mosaics. In the town you will also find Roman remains (towers, gates and reconstructed walls) and a solidly impressive Gothic town hall.

If you find you have spent too much time exploring, then consider backtracking to have lunch at a bargain restaurant in **SPELLO**, 4km north of Foligno. This little place has tiny cobbled streets snaking along a

Etruscan artefact

narrow ridge offering fine hill views. All the churches have been Baroque'd up to the rafters, but some have interesting pictures and frescoes (Pinturicchio examples in the Baglioni chapel of Sta Maria Maggiore). There are also Roman gates — Porta Venere and the Porta Consolare, recently restored with its statues and tower. The statues came from the Roman theatre, whose ruins can be seen before the town. After a meal at the **Cacciatore** (a plain place, yet with good local dishes at very reasonable rates and also rooms, again simple yet adequate with their own showers), sit on the terrace and look at the views around Mount Subasio, or climb for a panorama to the belvedere.

From Bevagna, proceed south to the high-perched town of **MONTEFALCO**, known as the Balcony of Umbria because of the truly fantastic views you can obtain. The hill on which it stands allows views in every direction and for a long distance — you can see even farther from the tower of the *palazzo comunale* in the round Piazza della Repubblica, supposedly almost all of Umbria! The town has many fine buildings and churches with frescoes.

Continue south along this charming road which winds on for some distance until it arrives at one of the gems of Umbria, the ancient city and festival centre of **SPOLETO**. This is a magical city. Not very large (pop: 45,000), it is shadowed by a romantic castle (the Rocca) and spread around a gem of a cathedral. An agricultural centre it has many narrow streets and picturesque views and every year is host to the famous Festival of Two Worlds, which brings its name to the world each June. An ancient city, Spoletium as it was called, became a Roman colony in 242BC when its Etruscan period ended. There are many Roman remains including temples and theatres, and the churches both in and around the town are important — do try to see S. Gregorio Maggiore of the 12th century with its fine campanile on the Piazza Garibaldi. The duòmo itself, on a very beautiful square (particularly romantic during festival times when concerts are held here as the sun sets), has a splendid doorway and a Renaissance porch surrounded with mosaics. Inside are superb frescoes from Filippo Lippi and his son (the painter is buried here in a 15th-century tomb) and other works by Pinturicchio in the Eroli Chapel. Spoleto could easily take a couple of days to explore (there is a 14th-century bridge with Roman foundations and a loggia to view the valley of the river Ticino, among its unusual attractions), and there are good places to eat. On market days the Piazza del Mercato cries out for a camera with its displays of fruit and produce. You will find many attractive walks and unusual viewpoints from the narrow and sometimes stepped streets — from the upper stretch of the

Via del'Arringo a fine panorama is presented of the duòmo and the surrounding country. There are considerable stretches of walls and the remains of an amphitheatre. A good place to stay, if you prefer being with your transport, in a modern place, is the **Motel Agip** off the highway and there is a noted restaurant there too (0743-49340). Otherwise, note the little **Benedetti** restaurant, a typical local place that serves good specialities and Umbrian wines in a pleasant atmosphere (0743-62375). Very reasonable.

Return to the route the way you came heading left along 418 towards S. Giovanni di Baiano (turning just after you cross the railway). The road winds through wooded countryside towards **ACQUASPARTA** beside N3 bis. This little town has mineral springs for the treatment of arthritis and gout. There is a charming little palace of the 16th century, the Palazzo Cesi, with a pretty courtyard. Follow the road towards the town of Todi, leaving the main road, 3 bis, to the right as you enter its outskirts.

TODI (pop: 20,000) is a remarkable little hill town with numerous ancient buildings. Unfortunately, its main piazza is often choked with cars, which can make it difficult to appreciate the fine ensemble of buildings from the duòmo with its sweeping staircase and sparse, elegant façade, to the Palazzo dei Priori with the eagle of the commune in bronze. On the other side of the square are two palaces — del Capitano and del Popolo, elegantly Gothic. A walk around the old town brings you to Roman alcoves in the old market, and there are also Etruscan and medieval fortifications with gates. Fine views and also the ruined castle — from here you have a good impression of a striking Renaissance church, Santa Maria della Consolazione, in the valley below. This is a domed building, after the style of Bramante, in the form of a Greek cross, commenced in 1508. The little convent of San Francesco has a fine fresco over its chapel altar, and nearby is a charming brick cloister with views. On a hill on the edge of the town by the Piazza della Repubblica stands the tall, sombre church of S. Fortunato, its austere interior (three equal aisles) a good background for its frescoes. Most impressive, however, is its central doorway which has been sculpted with marvellous and slightly outrageous figures around its frame. When I was in Todi the beautiful Victorian theatre was being restored, a lush little bandbox of gilded balconies. Restaurant — try **Umbria** with its superb views over the countryside and with grilled meats and game on the menu (0758-82390).

The road meanders through wild countryside west towards Orvieto, but a pleasing detour can be made by turning to the right just after leaving Todi on 79 bis. This road, 397, takes you along the valley of the Tiber towards the village of **MARSCIANO** where there is an impressive ruined castle, and farther on to **CERQUETO** if you wish, where the church has a fresco that will be of interest if you are planning to explore Perugia and view the painter's house, for here is one of Perugino's earliest works, a Saint Sebastian. Return to the main route via 317, meandering through the Umbrian hills to arrive at Colonetta. If you drive straight from Todi keep on the winding 79 bis with its views (note the castle at **PRODO**) as the theatrical outline of Orvieto crowning an impressive plug of volcanic tufa looms ahead. It is one of the most grandly placed of towns, the drive up the sides of the mount indicating what an impregnable fortress it must have been in antiquity.

ORVIETO (pop: 25,000) was the famed Velsina of the Etruscan league, but the Romans took it and the inhabitants moved to Bolsena on its lake, forming associations between the two settlements. A papal stronghold under the Guelph party in the 12th century, it was for long a part of the Papal States. Its name has evolved from the Roman *Urbs Vetus*. There are many Etruscan remains (tombs and a temple on the way up the hill) and at the point where the principal entry road arrives at the plateau there is a noted well designed by Sangallo and known as the *pozzo di San Patrizio*. A fine double staircase descends to the water 64m below. Near the tower marking the well is the public garden and the remnants of the *fortezza* with excellent views over the wide valley.

The cathedral is one of the most beautiful in Italy, designed and supervised by the master architect, Maitani, who sculpted the marvellous façade. The new cathedral was constructed after a miraculous occurrence in Bolsena, when it was reported by a doubting priest that the host had bled after the consecration. The napkin is conserved in a silver reliquary in the Chapel of the Corporale, shown only on Corpus Domini. The cathedral is beautifully sited at the head of a flight of shallow steps and the façade is a striking balance of elements incorporating sculpture in relief and in the round, in marble and in bronze, mosaics and a fine rose window set in a square by Orcagna. Inside it is austerely beautiful and unobstructed. The most famous frescoes are those by Signorelli, in the Cappella Nuova, based on the day of judgment.

Outside the cathedral in a rather dusty and ramshackle museum are treasures from the duòmo, situated in the 13th-century Palace of the Popes (enter by the external stair). Etruscan finds are in the nearby Palazzo Faina — some superb sculptures and pottery. A charming little church lit with alabaster windows is S. Andrea, with a campanile and frescoes; an undercroft contains Roman and Etruscan foundations and sculpture. Near the entrance to the Piazza del Duòmo is a 14th-century clocktower with a figure striking the hours. No visit to Orvieto should overlook the possibilities of a walk along the crooked little streets with views over the surrounding countryside constantly offered. It is also a good idea to try the wines — mostly white, with *Est Est Est* a favourite. A reasonable restaurant is **Del Pino da Cecco** with its interior garden (0763-35381). At the foot of the hill is the Abbey of Sts Severo and Martirio, with a fine 12-sided campanile which is now a smart restaurant in part. A grand hotel is the ancient **La Badia** with garden and pool.

Drive north from here on 71 towards Ficulle and Citta della Pieve, but our route turns right here on 220 to Perugia. [A detour up to CITTÀ DELLA PIEVE is well worthwhile, however, for this little city has some fine works by Perugino who was born here in 1445. The duòmo has restored works, and Sta. Maria dei Bianchi has a fresco of the Adoration of the Magi. The road to Perugia is more direct than the undulating one from Orvieto, and takes you across the hills towards the village of **FONTIGNANO** with its castle and a little church where Perugino is buried — there is also a fresco of his. From this road there are good views over the shallow waters of Lake Trasimeno with its islands. You can take boats to the three isles from Passignano (off the first Umbrian route) and an interesting excursion from this route is to **CASTIGLIONE DEL LAGO** on the western shore — a charmingly sited little place with a castle on a point and superb views all around — you could do this from Citta della Pieve returning by a lakeside road, 599, to arrive at Perugia.] Continuing through the hills the main route crosses the railway and the autostrada and climbs up Perugia's prominent hill to arrive back at the starting point.

North from Perugia

1 day or longer/200km

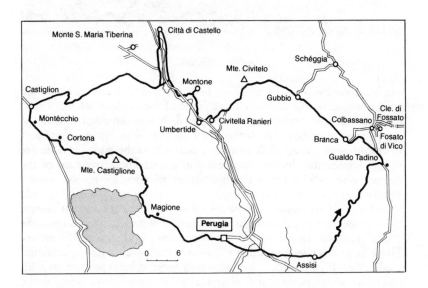

From Perugia take the steep road down towards the N3, thence following the signs for Foligno. At the intersection with the N75 continue on a short distance until Collestrada when you will turn left on the 147 for **ASSISI** (pop: 24,000) reached at a distance of 12km. This is a popular town, of course, and it is wise to start this particular ride early to get to the pilgrimage town before the crowds, since you should leave your vehicle and walk, even though it does mean steep streets especially if you start, as you ought, at the top of the town.

There is a fine view from the hilltop Rocca Maggiore but this does entail a very steep climb and the views from around the Roman

View of Assisi

amphitheatre are very good. From here descend into the close-packed town along beautiful streets to the Duòmo of San Rufino, where Assisi's most famous son, St Francis, was baptised. It is a cathedral with a fine aspect and the exterior is elegant; grandly bare with three magnificent wheel windows and heraldic beasts on each side of the portal. The inside is late 16th-century renovation, but the architectural grouping of the exterior with its 11th-century campanile set above a sloping courtyard is very fine.

In the centre of the town, the *piazza communale*, is the spectacular Temple of Minerva, with its six Corinthian columns (now a church). Nearby is the art gallery, contained in a 14th-century building and with early frescoes. There is an excellent restaurant nearby, offering Umbrian specialities, **Medio Evo** (075-813068). So venerated was St Francis that even his family home is encased in a church, but the main attraction for the pilgrims is the vast double basilica at the east end of the little town. Here you will find the tomb of the saint and frescoes by followers of Giotto (lower church), while in the Gothic upper church, an architectural surprise after the sombre one below, you will find the famous 28 frescoes by Giotto himself as well as others by Cimabue. There are many shops in the town selling an assortment of tourist junk and religious statuettes, but you might care to look for the local embroidery.

If you wish to discover more of the saint, take a short detour to the Eremo Carceri, a church cut out of the rock which St Francis once used to visit to pray supposedly in the grotto. The Hermitage is set in densely wooded hills, about 6km from the town and its terrace has fine views; but if you really want a grand overview continue on this narrow road to Mt Subasio.

From Assisi we head on the 444 towards Gualdo Tadino (signposted). The road goes through hilly country, rapidly leaving the wide and fertile Valle Umbra behind. You could ask for no more Italian a landscape than this as the valleys reveal ravishing views and sometimes whole ranks of blue hills fold one behind the other, while the agriculture is often in long strips lined with vines and olives on the hillsides. Settlements are small. Sometimes no more than a couple of red-tiled houses. You reach the 318 at Cerqueto and turn right — you can cut up on a backroad to the left to the 219, but it would be a pity not to take time to view the old city of **GUALDO TADINO**. It is famed for its so-called artistic pottery, but the town itself on its high hilltop roost is a place of much charm with narrow cobbled streets and the looming 14th-century castle.

The road from Gualdo starts as the busy N3 but you rapidly turn left onto the 219 marked for Gubbio, or you can continue up the N3 to **COLBASSANO**, a junction on the road beside the old town of **FOSSATO DI VICO**, where there are ruins and fortifications. The road to Gubbio cuts off to the left towards Branca, but if you wish to see the Fossato Pass at 755m heading towards Fabriano in the Marches, take the N76 and branch off at a tiny road to the left for views down to the valley.

Returning to the 219 continue straight along until you see in the distance the terraced houses of **GUBBIO** (pop: 31,400). This compact hill-town is one of the most fascinating in Italy, and offers many things to see. Standing against a green, cliff-like hill, Gubbio seems almost like a toytown with its turrets and towers. It is the perfect place to stop for an afternoon, or longer. Park at the lower part of the little *citta* and walk up to the grand terrace above the roofs for a wide-flung prospect of the hills of the Eugobino countryside. The city is an ancient religious centre, and Eugobium to the Romans. Don't miss the Piazza della Signoria, where you will find the Palazzo dei Consoli (14th century) which also contains the art gallery (open mornings and afternoons) where you will see examples of Gubbio's pottery and a set of bronze tablets from the 3rd century BC. Also to be viewed are the Duòmo, the Ducal Palace built by Federico, duke of Urbino in the 15th century, and medieval houses along the Via Baldassini just below the piazza where some still have two doorways — the lower one 'for the dead'. The principal pleasure of this town, however, is the simple one of walking ancient streets where people still live; while busy in summer Gubbio is not as infested with tourists as are some better-known towns. There are good restaurants around the Piazza Quaranta Martiri at the foot of the town (park and walk from here) and every year on 15 May there is a vast procession, the *corsa dei Ceri*, when St Ubaldo, one-time bishop, is given a grand medieval revival. You can walk up to his chapel at Mont' Ingino. It stands above the town and has wonderful views. The chapel can also be reached by car — drive towards Scheggia and turn right at Fornarette up the mountainside. The road on to Scheggia follows a steep-sided and picturesque valley.

Umbrian vineyards

The 219 continues from Gubbio down the valley of the river Assino towards Umbertide. On the left look out for **CIVITELLA RANIERI**, a splendid castle with towers and ramparts framed in woods. About 4km farther on you arrive beside the river Tiber. Here, at the junction of the highway (the western branch, marked as 3 bis on maps), is the small atmospheric town of **UMBERTIDE**. Here is a wonderful castle, *La Rocca*, brick-built and with both round and square towers, turreted and crenellated. The castle is 14th century and yes, there are dungeons too. In the church of Santa Croce is a picture by Signorelli. In this *alta valle del Tevere* there are spreads of arable land between low hills intensively cultivated with crops including tobacco and vines as well as groves of ancient olive trees.

From Umbertide take the tiny road north to **MONTONE** (8km). Here you will find a fine church set in a little fortified hill-town of great charm. Descend down a winding road to the 3 bis and turn right for **CITTÀ DI CASTELLO** (about 13km). This little settlement spreads itself comfortably on Tiber's bank with low hills in the background. It possesses several good buildings, including a cathedral with an unusual 16th-century interior — not a Baroque ballroom for a change, but elegantly Renaissance. Another building in the town of the same epoch is the Palazzo Vitelli. There is an art gallery with star-name pictures, but worth a visit is the folk and country art museum at **GARAVELLE**. Here you can see how local people lived with furnished period rooms and costumes and implements, all naturally presented in authentic settings. In this area fabrics are still produced using the old techniques. From Citta di Castello cross the Tiber and head south on the companion road to the highway across the valley. At S. Secondo a road to the right will take you the 15km to **MONTE S. MARIA TIBERINA**, a perfect little town clustered tightly around its hilltop church, maintaining a medieval aspect. At Trestina turn right and follow a long and fairly direct rural road to **CASTIGLIONE**, a distance of 35km. Half-way along you cross into Tuscany. Castiglion Fiorentino, to give it its full name, is a town serving local agricultural holdings, but besides the shops it has several fine churches and also some of its original town walls.

From here take the main N71 south a short distance to Cortona past the castle of Montecchio to the left (ruined 11th-century structure) then look for signs to the left for **CORTONA**. This is intriguing in that it was an Etruscan town, a major centre for these mysterious early Tuscans. Here were born several painters, notably Lucca Signorelli in the mid-15th century. There is a gallery with works of Signorelli and others in the Palazzo Pretoria, which also contains a museum of Etruscan art (open every day, closed lunchtimes). Other paintings can be seen in the Diocesan Museum of the mainly 15th-century duòmo. The city is extremely attractive, set on a hillside and with steeply inclined streets, often arched and with flights of steps. There are attractive public gardens with views as far as Lake Trasimeno which is easily reached from here down the N71.

We, however, will pursue a narrow rural road towards Sta Maria beneath Mte Castiglione on the border of Umbria. This road continues to loop through fine scenery necessitating careful driving until the little town of **CASTEL RIGONE**, about 28km from Cortona. There are fine views but best of all a strikingly beautiful Renaissance church, the Madonna dei Miracoli. The interior of this late 15th-century building contains frescoes. A ruined castle adds to the romantic air of this pleasant town. For about 3km the road edges the lake until Torricella, where it crosses the new autostrada and arrives at **MAGIONE** with its old stronghold of the Knights of Malta.

Rising away from the lake the road continues towards Perugia, beside the autostrada 75 bis.

7 TUSCANY
(Toscana)

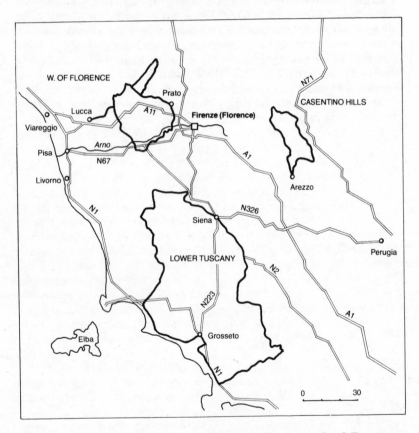

Tuscany has always exerted a powerful pull for the civilised European. Here, in this ancient land of mountain and olive tree, facing the vivid blue of the Mediterranean from a long and varied coast, civilisations have been born and the great spirit of the Renaissance first started. It is a place to spend a long time, not a few harried days, and these routes are admittedly long. If you have the time and do not wish to treat this marvellous country ungenerously, plan to follow the routes in slow motion, stopping where you will, and extending them too. There is so much to see and so many alluring places to visit.

The great cities spring to mind, with Florence (Italian: Firenze), a lion on a lily-bed, resplendent in the middle of the region. Yet although a magnet and not to be overlooked, it is hot and dusty in summer and, to be honest, overcrowded. Like Venice, it might be better to visit from an outside base. There are many choices of unusual towns to visit in Tuscany, and most will have good hotels and at least one fine restaurant. Consider, in addition to the bases suggested, stopping in San Gimignano, in Montecatini, in Pisa, in Lucca, in Grosseto — or in any of many small seaside places or hill villages.

Adopt the pace of the Florentines and do things elegantly and slowly, Sometimes the perfect charm of Tuscany comes not from great monuments or museums but from a sudden vista, a combination of scenic elements, a simple village street. Tuscany has so much to offer and even when you think you have discovered the secrets still some are held back — for return. A region both ancient and modern, Tuscany still has the power to stop you — and surprise.

The Casentino Hills
1 day or longer/about 160km/from Arezzo

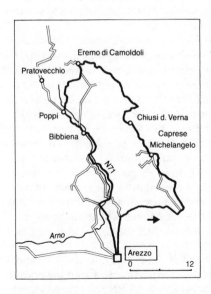

Arezzo makes an excellent centre for exploring this small and yet fascinating hill mass which embraces both upper valleys of the Arno and the Tiber. It is a secret country, approached by steeply climbing roads once you leave the long north-south valleys where major roads will take you on to Florence or to Perugia.

The town of **AREZZO** (pop: 87,000) is very old, indeed it pre-dates Rome, and the classical name to summon up riches of wildest dreams was born here — Maecenas, along with others luminous in other fields — Petrarch and Vasari, with Michelangelo coming from a small town not far off, Caprese, which this route takes in. Arezzo is a city built on a slope of the Apennines, deep in Tuscany, yet very close to Umbria and the Marches. It was an early city-state, rich and prosperous up until the end of the medieval period when it became vassal to Florence, although the town did not lose its importance. Every year on the Piazza Grande, a cobbled incline surrounded by striking buildings, the Saracens' Joust takes place and is preceded by a procession (usually the first Sunday of June).

Arezzo well repays a walk before venturing out on the road. Around the Piazza Grande explore the fine church of Sta Maria with a harmonious arched apse facing the square and an arcaded front at the west end of the church, at which point rises the massive square belltower; its severe Romanesque aspect makes it a landmark. This four-tiered façade is worth looking at in detail. The many pillars are all different, but you may need the aid of a pair of binoculars to see the details. Next is the Laymen's Guild, a Gothic palace with a later belltower and, along one side of the square, the wide arches of the Palazzo delle Logge. There is a 15th-century well with a roof, once the public water supply. The plain rather spartan cathedral is on the Piazza della Liberta. It is a mixture of periods, started in the 13th century and contains in the Lady chapel terracottas of della Robbia. On the other side of the piazza is the impressive towered Palazzo dei Priori, its plain façade enlivened with the fish-tailed turrets so often seen here. There are several interesting churches to visit, notably S. Francesco with frescoes by Piero della Francesca (Legend of the Cross), and Sta. Maria delle Grazie, about 2km from the centre, notable for its elegant Renaissance portico by Benedetto da Maiano, and an altar by della Robbia in marble and terracotta. Both Petrarch's and Vasari's houses still exist, and besides the turreted walls earlier origins can be seen at the site of the Roman theatre, of the first century BC, although the remains are minimal.

From Arezzo you will need to take a small road which parallels for a time the main N71 towards Chiassa and Anghiari — don't be dismayed if you miss it, for there are several connecting roads to the right from the N71 towards the range of hills known as the Alpe di Catenaia, part of the main mass of the Casentino Hills which enwrap you like the folds of a cloak. After Chiassa (8km) head over the hills via the Valico di Scheggia, after which you can coast to Anghiari (14km). It is possible to continue towards our next objective on a narrow backroad to the left (towards tiny Ponte alla Piero) but the better road is from Anghiari to the village of **CAPRESE MICHELANGELO**. This is the painter's home town, a little place in the green sweep of the hills, and well worth a stop. Here you can see and visit his birthplace, a severe little stone house where Michelangelo Buonarroti was born in 1470 — it has been well restored and is easy to find.

As is not uncommon here several small roads run into the hills and have no outlet — still they make interesting explorations. Continue north another 12km and you will come to **CHIUSI D. VERNA**, staged along its rocky spur. This is a place of particular interest to the followers of St Francis, for the saint first set up small wattle-and-daub huts here with his disciples. Here he also visited a grotto, where in 1224 he supposedly received the stigmata — the spot is now marked with a chapel (every

Della Robia sculpture

place the saint visited seems to have been subsequently built over) and a plaque is set into the floor. The simple little stone building with its tower and plain arched porticoes is quietly impressive, however, and less grandiose than some later constructions such as the Baroque palace of Santa Maria degli Angeli which covers the saint's homely chapel at Assisi.

All around the sanctuary of La Verna are deep woods. Continue on to Badia Prataglia, over the main (but steeply winding) 208 towards Bibbiena. You will pass through the forest of Camaldoli, beech trees on the lower slopes and massed firs and larches as you ascend, until you come to the remote Hermitage. Here, at the **EREMO DI CAMALDOLI**, is a monastery of the 11th century in a forest clearing. Twenty cells inhabited by monks surround a Baroque church which has a magnificent aspect. A little higher and you come to the **PRATO DEL SOGLIO**, which has wide-ranging views over the range of Apennines — a spectacular sight — a good place to plan a stop and maybe a picnic, though you may need to seek a sheltered spot.

Return from the Hermitage down to **Camaldoli** itself, a health spa with advantages of forest air. Its monastery, founded in 1012 by St Romuald, has works by Vasari and Mina da Fieseole in its 16th-century church. Here you have a choice — you can descend by a longer road to Bibbiena, by-passing Poppi, or else go down a picturesque mountain road via Maggiona to **POPPI**, a small town (pop: about 10,000) situated on the upper valley of the river Arno. Here you may join the N70 (later N71) for eventual return to Arezzo, although it is possible, if you are eager to explore the Casentino in more detail, to make detours off these main roads. [It is worth going on to **PRATOVECCHIO**, where Dante is supposed to have lived at the castello, and a little farther up the Arno's valley to **STIA**, where there is an impressive 12th-century church with a della Robbia holy family. Beyond, a new road will take you on up to the ski resort village of **PASSO LA CALLA**, a distance of about 25km from the centrally placed Poppi.] Poppi itself is recommended as a place to stop and explore: it still has its town walls, having once been an important capital of the region, and whilst it now only has the remnants of past glories they are grand indeed — the castle of the Counts Guidi is a stern

13th-century place, handsomely sited and with a tower over its battlemented and decorated walls — inside the castle; the exterior is bare but the courtyard provides an impressive parade of coats of arms. This is the birthplace of the 15th-century artist, Mina da Fiesole.

Just south of Poppi is Bibbiena, a similar sized yet less picturesque town, but a good centre for shops. Continue down the N71 and, if you have time, you can make detours on the parallel roads as you descend the valley of the Arno and arrive back at the starting point of Arezzo.

Lower Tuscany
3 days/about 500km/from Siena

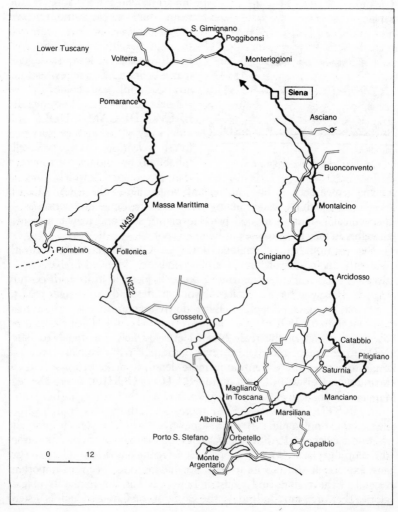

Although for many **SIENA** (pop: 67,000) is reason enough to travel to Tuscany, it has a limited charm. Some Tuscan towns invite return, Siena does not in my estimation. It has fascinating buildings, a famous cathedral and town hall with a superbly fine square, the shell-shaped Piazza del Campo with the lean brick shaft of the Torre del Mangia complementing it like an exclamation mark, yet the city has a cold atmosphere. You can well believe that these people held back on Donatello's fee for his work at the cathedral (an amazing John the Baptist and sculptures on the façade) for the Sienese had a reputation for being hard and businesslike. They also made their city on a steep hill a very grand one, the ornateness of the buildings seems almost 19th century at times; they were the Victorians of their age, although they failed miserably to aggrandise the cathedral. As you stand in the Piazza del Duòmo you can see the arches of a vast structure, for which the present large building would have been but a transept. The plague stopped Sienese ambitions, probably to the relief of later prelates — such a building would be staggeringly expensive to maintain and far larger than the city's population merited. The present cathedral is the first of the Tuscan Gothic, despite Romanesque origins, and contains many treasures. The three-part façade lacks proportion, but is a spectacular creation with its elegant campanile beside it, banded in white and black. The interior is so overloaded with sculpture and ornamentation it hovers perilously close to the vulgar at times, were it not for the fine quality of individual works — note the Pisano pulpit and the engraved floors — the original 'graffiti'. Try to visit the Piccolomini Library, a charming Renaissance room with frescoes by Pinturicchio. Outside the building go around to the Piazza San Giovanni and look at the Baptistery with its beautiful marble font. There are many palaces along the three main streets of the city — you could spend a couple of days just walking around and identifying them, but look for the Palazzo Buonsignori which contains the Pinacotèca, where all the great early Sienese masters can be studied. You can follow trails of the saints Catherine and Bernardino around the town. The famous *Palio* is contested each year in the town (2 July and 16 August) between the 17 *contrade* or districts of Siena. It is preceded with parades and flag-throwing and the horse-race itself is watched by huge crowds clustering the piazza and the balconies of the elegant palaces facing the Palazzo Pubblico. It is probably something in my own character that finds Siena overbearing and inbred, but I find I long to get back to the cool Renaissance pleasures of Florence after Siena's excesses. The **Minerva Hotel** on the Via Garibaldi is a good, plain hotel whilst the restaurant, **Al Mangia**, has good pasta and game (577-281121).

From Siena, take the main road towards Colle di Val d'Elsa. It's a road offering some remarkable sights — principally the view of **MONTERIGGIONI**, a complete medieval village on a hill. The sight of it as you approach creates a most romantic feeling, for the walls are complete and the 14 towers still stand, dating from the 13th century. It is mentioned in Dante's *Inferno*, but now the stern fortifications enclose a quiet settlement where nothing seems to happen at all, yet the sense of having moved back in time is intense. A lovely spot for a picnic!

The road continues through hilly scenery (note turnoff to the right for the village of **STAGGIA** where you will find more fortifications (ruinous) and a 15th-century Rocca: continue on backroads to Poggibonsi if wished, avoiding Colle) until it arrives at the birthplace of the great 13th-century architect, Arnolfo di Cambio whose tower house can be seen in the town. **COLLE DI VAL D'ELSA** is a good place to stop and explore on foot: there is much to see including the walls and ancient houses ranged along the Via del Castello. Colle is set along the ridge of a hill: it has a long main street running across a bridge (fine views) into the old town, the Castello. There are several museums including the Antiquarium in the Piazza del Duòmo, where you can see finds from a nearby necropolis. In the Palazzo Vescovile are frescoes and religious pictures. In the lower part of town, Col Basso, there is an unfinished church, San Agostino, with unusual pictures including a Bronzino. Continue on the road north for 7km to **POGGIBONSI** (pop: 30,000), where there are grandly sited ruins — the castle of Poggio Imperiale on a hill just south of the town. It's worth stopping to visit the monastery of S. Lucchese with its frescoes.

A small road, heading west, goes to **SAN GIMIGNANO**, one of the finest survivals in Italy of a town of the Middle Ages. Allow plenty of time to visit this atmospheric town, which appears thrusting its famous towers into the sky as you ascend the road from Poggibonsi. It was San Gimignano's good fortune to wane in importance after the takeover of its

Tower of San Gimignano

assets by Florence in 1533, and to remain much as it was then — although of the angular towers the 13 now standing are but the remnant of 70 which once marked the warfare between the Guelph and the Ghibelline parties. Whatever the weather it is always a good idea to climb the *Torre Grossa* and scan the countryside — I recall doing this during a rainstorm (be prepared for a precipitous climb up the interior stairs) and being rewarded at the top with a sparkling view making the countryside look like a painting of the 15th century. There is an art gallery and the interior of the cathedral is a wonder after the severe exterior — round, striped arches with painted vaults, and gleaming frescoes in bright colours banded along the walls. Be sure to save small change from purchases for operating the lights — 100 and 200 lire pieces are always useful. The square of the Cisterna gets its name from the stepped public fountain — and here is as good a place as any in this marvellous town to sit and enjoy a drink while savouring a remarkable survivor of another era. **Hotel La Cisterna** is an excellent place to stay, and the restaurant, **La Terrazze**, is locally renowned (0577-940328) and shares the amazing views of the little town and the surrounding hills.

From San Gimignano a little road curves through Camporbiano (alternative road to the right, if wished, down to 439 dir) a distance of about 23km to N439 where you turn right and continue towards **VOLTERRA**. The surrounding countryside is undulating and enriched with the scent of oleander and evergreens, a soft bucolic frame for the sudden high hill on which this compact city stands. Ancient walls, round towers and red tiles lend it a sparse, almost bald air and mark it as a medieval fortified town, but it is much older than that. It was actually the Etruscan city of Velathri, much larger than the later city, and famous as one of the 12 cities of the Etrurian league. Many reminders of the long-gone Etruscans remain, however, and you can find a famous Etruscan gate, a museum of artifacts (open mornings and afternoons, except Mon; the Guarnacci is on Via Minzoni) and well-defined walls. The town was for a time the seat of the Lombards; later it became vassal to Florence in the mid-14th century. The town itself, once entered, is narrow and cramped and yet still commands marvellous views in every direction across the hilly countryside around. The limestone used for many of the buildings (called *panchina* is local and is often embedded with alabaster. This is used extensively for the making of statuettes and artifacts, so you will find many souvenirs of the fine stone. Look for the Palazzo dei Priori (town hall), built in the 13th century and the oldest building of its kind in the region. The duòmo is much restored and internally redesigned, but the campanile is good, and there is a charming 12th-century baptistery. Along the Via Ricciarelli are good tower houses, and the great Arco Etrusco complete with the fragments of three giant Etruscan heads should not be missed (Roman restoration). There is a Roman bath and theatre (mosaics). Lorenzo the Magnificent supervised the building of the Fortezza, a keep and corner towers, now a prison. In Volterra there is a very good restaurant, in a palace — the **Etruria** (0588-86064), where you can sample local cooking.

From Volterra, the N68 takes you onwards (look back for fine views of the town) until you arrive at **SALINE DI VOLTERRA**, where there are indeed salt mines. Take N439 to **POMARANCE**, the birthplace of two painters of the name and a pleasant town — fortified and with good palaces. [Roads to the right will take you to the coast where there are pleasant resorts among the pines, and also the seaport of **LIVORNO** (pop: 190,000), once known as Leghorn. It was much destroyed in bombardments of 1943, so few old buildings remain, but it is an agreeable modern town and its duòmo has a portico originally designed by Inigo Jones. Tobias Smollett is buried in the old English cemetery. It is the birthplace of the painter Modigliani and the composer Mascagni.]

N439 takes you on down towards Massa past **LARDERELLO**, where jets bursting from underground provide an industry producing boric acid, and so over the pass of Aia dei Diavoli into the town of **MASSA MARITTIMA**, which was once an independent republic and still has fine walls. It has a plethora of 13th-century buildings, and you should stop to see the cathedral of San Cerbone which although plain outside contains much good sculpture and pictures within, notably a font of the 13th century with carved reliefs. Leave the lower town for the upper or 'new' town where there are castle ruins (Sienese and earlier) and a museum at the School of Mines which illustrates the metal ores found in the local hills and how they are used.

The hills are left far behind as you continue along N439 across a wide shelf of land ending in **FOLLONICA**, a small town with a good sand beach and views over the gulf of the same name, towards the **Isle of Elba**.

If you wish to visit **ELBA**, or the promontory you can see from Follonica, turn right in the town and take the sea-front road to the north, then a short detour on the main N1 and turn left at signs to **PIOMBINO**. This little town on a point, the Masoncello peninsula, was once cut off by the sea, and is now a ferry port dominated by ugly smelting works.

From here ferry boats go to Elba (from the Porto Vecchio) but you will need at least a couple of days to enjoy the island properly — the ferry to Portoferraio takes about 90 minutes. There is a faster but more expensive hydrofoil service to the island; services are more frequent in summer. Don't expect a serene little place — there is plenty of industry around **PORTOFERRAIO**, an ordinary port with huge blast furnaces dominating it — the fortress is interesting, built on the side of the promontory, overlooking the Gulf. Much of the island is rocky and the coast is deeply indented with mountains inland. A tour of the western part of the island will show you the Napoleonic connection — his country residence is known as Villa di Napoleone and contains relics and mementos as well as period furnishings. Another residence of the emperor is in the main town, the Villetta dei Mulini, by the sea at Portoferraio. It has been preserved as it was in Napoleon's time and there are souvenirs of the period. The gardens offer charming views and one has a statue of Galatea, posed for by the emperor's sister, Pauline. Elba's scenery varies from the picturesque to the barren and exposed, and there are several attractive coast resorts around its shores.

From Piombino an excursion to the port of the Etruscans, **POPULONIA**, will show something of the life of these mysterious peoples — the village has walls and there is a necropolis and a small museum. Nearby is a picturesque castle of much later date, a *rocca* with round towers of the 14th century.

The route continues with 322 south towards Grosseto, but you can make an interesting excursion along a rough road towards the rocks of Punta Ala. This is wild country, even though cultivated. There are camping sites and good walks. Continue along the inland arm of the road (N322) to **CASTIGLIONE DELLA PESCAIA**, a resort on the site of a Roman town, walled and with a castle. You are in the middle of the Maremma district: extensive pinewoods surround the next town, **MARINA DI GROSSETO**, which has a wide and sandy beach. A short drive along the road leading inland will take you to Grosseto itself. [Alternatively you could have taken a backroad route from Castiglione to **VETULONIA** and a visit to the Etruscan city of Vetluna, where are preserved a street of houses and a necropolis, and some distance off is a rare tomb.]

GROSSETO (pop: 75,000) is an old town, the capital of its province and of the Maremma. There is a 12th-century cathedral and the battlemented walls provide a very pleasant walk whilst the arcades of the Piazza Dante provide a place for a cool stroll when the sun is too hot. There is an archaeological museum, open every day except Wednesdays, showing Etruscan remains including a fascinating vase carrying the letters of the Etruscan alphabet. For local cooking of the Maremma, including roast meats, try the small and central **Canepone** (0564-24546) which offers very reasonable meals and game in season.

From Grosseto follow the road (N1) down the coast towards the impressive bulk of Monte Argentario. [Or you could penetrate inland after crossing the valley of the Ombrone, at first following a rural road towards **MAGLIANO IN TOSCANA,**, with walls and old churches near an Etruscan burial ground, then turning north-east along N323 to rejoin the route much farther on after a long and tortuous drive.] The main route continues right at Rispescia along a little road by the river valley. It leads to the sea, and also to the heavily wooded **Monte Dell' Uccellina** made into a national park in the 1970s and with only tracks and paths, so to explore you will need to walk. You can, however, drive to the coast and park your car, then walk to the ruins of the abbey of San Rabano, and perhaps continue on to the romantic remains of the Torre della Bella Marsilia. Pirates destroyed the defences 4½ centuries ago and carried off the beautiful daughter of the Marsili family to be sold into the harem of a Sultan whom she later married and became chief wife. Continuing until the road rejoins the main road south, and after traversing the river Albegna you will come straightaway to a left turn at Albinia where R74 heads towards Manciano. A fascinating diversion may be made around

Tuscany

the neighbouring peninsula, however, along a road bordering a lagoon towards Porto S. Stefano (departures by boat for the Island of Giglio). From here you can drive all around the mountain on its peninsula — Monte Argentario is impressive and its slopes end in rocky bays and little beaches. You can return to the mainland along the south arm (there are three, called *tomboli*) through the pines, or visit ORBETELLO, which is the focus of a smart beach area, the Costa Argenta. The town itself possesses some fine monuments notably a handsome duòmo with a 14th-century front and a curious Spanish building, the *polverièra*, left after an early occupation. Orbetello is in the middle of the lagoon and there are good views back to the outline of Monte Argentario. Continue on this central isthmus to Orbetello Scala and turn left to rejoin the route at Albinia where you turn right for Manciano on N74.

[An alternative route from Monte Argentario is to take the southern arm, the Tombolo di Feniglia, arriving where it meets the main coast at a curious flat-topped hillock. Here stood the city of Cosa, a Roman settlement. If you stop and climb the hill you will find a wall and towers; within are Roman remains including a temple. The town is now called ANSEDONIA and is marked thus on maps. It is a pleasing little place encircling the hill and with a good beach. Cross N1 here and follow directions for CAPALBIO, an ancient village surrounded by a game reserve. Now you have a choice of two country roads running north to join the Albenga valley, and N74. Turn right through Marsiliana for Manciano.]

[As another possible interesting deviation, from Manciano turn left on N322, first to MONTERMERANO, a walled town, and then to the right a rural road will take you to the spa of SATURNIA with ancient walls and ramparts. Continue on to join the main route near Catabbio.] The route itself, N74, continues on the main road to PITIGLIANO. This is a small wine-producing town, where you can sample wine while looking at the old palace of the Orsini. Turn north outside the town on a twisting road to SOVANA, a town of impressive ruins. It was once much bigger, and based on an Etruscan town — there is a necropolis — which has now dwindled to a village. The atmosphere is decidedly strange and sad — it was the birthplace of a pope, and the impressive church ruins tell the tale. The road winds on to Catabbio, then Triana where N323 joins it (end of suggested alternate route via Magliano in Toscana). At Arcidosso leave the main road and head left towards Cinigiano, where it makes a right turn and continues on via Falsettaio to MONTALCINO. This is a splendid little town and the home of a famous wine, known throughout Italy — the Brunello, robust yet delicate — do try it and buy a bottle or two to take home! The town is walled, has a spacious castle which each year presents spectacles in its courtyard, and possesses charming cobbled streets of houses where you can buy local honey and folk crafts. There are two museums (Sienese primitive paintings and wooden carvings, as well as archaeological remains) and a pleasant square to take your ease in. Nearby a great abbey, the church of Sant'Antimo, rises above the woods and neighbouring hills. The inside glows in a magical way from the

90

alabaster construction of the mainly 12th-century church — some parts, including two doorways, are even earlier.

Continue along the road marked for **BUONCONVENTO** at a junction of roads on the Ombrone river. This place has a museum of Sienese primitives and is notable as the site of Emperor Henry VII's death. It is a handsome town with ramparts and very grand gates. Inside it is cramped and medieval in pattern, decidedly picturesque. To the north-east is the monastery of Monte Oliveto Maggiore, high on a hill. It is actually a large group of buildings occupied by monks of the order of the Olivetans, a Benedictine branch. You can be shown around and look especially for the great cloister with frescoes by Sodoma and Signorelli, the small cloister, and the tour also takes you to the pharmacy and the refectory. The monks make their own liqueur and pottery, which can be purchased at a shop.

Return to join the main road towards Siena. Another excursion a little farther on the right will take you to **ASCIANO**, a town perched up on a high point of the Ombrone Valley with a fine church on its main piazza, S. Agata, with an impressive octagonal cupola. The town wall dates from the 14th century. Return down the valley to the main road at Monteroni d'Arbia and turn right — the road will take you directly back to your starting point and a good view of the skyline of Siena.

West of Florence
1 day or more/160km/from Prato

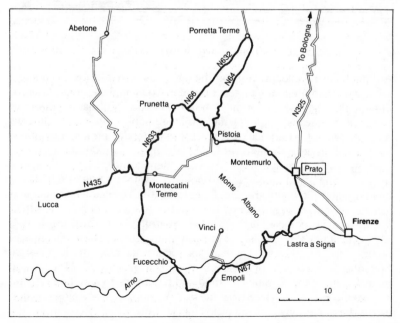

Santa Croce, Florence

Although Florence looms large on the map, it is perhaps wiser to choose a smaller town to use as a base for this route. You could use either Prato or Pistoia, although the former might be a better choice in that it is closer to Florence and means that you could easily use public transport to slip into this great city of art and culture which has figured so prominently in the history of European thought. **FLORENCE** (pop: 500,000, Italian name: Firenze) reached its apogee in the early Renaissance, being called 'the Italian Athens', and much of it is unchanged with a range of superlative buildings giving the city grace and elegance. It has so many museums and galleries that an adequate period to do justice to them can be no less than five days. Being compact it is easily walked around, and the central city is still occupied by the premises of artists and artisans so that it is lively and often a delight to the eye. There are excellent restaurants (try **Le Quattro Stagione**; 055-218906, or a bargain place, **La Spada**, 055-218757) and many hotels — the **Regency** is grand and has a very good restaurant, and the **Mediterraneo** is placed beside the Arno. Excellent transportation across the rather ugly built-up plain towards Prato.

PRATO (pop: 155,000) is a manufacturing town, yet it still preserves a fine old centre and is beside the autostrada to the airport for Florence at Pisa. Although probably Etruscan in origin, Prato achieved note as a wool town in the Middle Ages. Textiles are still the major industry. In the city you will find some fine buildings, notably a 13th-century castle with ramparts, several churches (often containing good pictures) and a striped marble duòmo with a very fine belltower. It has a pulpit by Donatello with reliefs by Michelozzo, and the Chapel of the Sacred Girdle, as well as many art works. In the Museum (beside the old cloister) are the original Donatello reliefs from the pulpit. There is a gallery of pictures in the *Palazzo Pretorio*, which stands close to the arcaded *palazzo del comune*. Behind S. Maria della Carceri, one of the great works of the Renaissance (its interior should not be missed) is the very fine Teatro Comunale Metastio with early 19th-century décor. A highly regarded local restaurant (moderately expensive) is **Il Piranha** (0574-25746).

Take the old road out of Prato towards Pistoia, a distance of 20km, and stop to look at the charming castle of **MONTEMURLO**, where in 1537 plotters met to try to overthrow the Medicis of Florence. On the other road, N66, going direct from Pistoia to Florence is **POGGIO A CAIANO** where Lorenzo di Medici's villa is situated below Monte Albano. You can make an interesting itinerary from Prato to Bologna, through dramatic scenery and wild hills along the Bisenzio valley.

PISTOIA (pop: 100,000) is a handsome and important town, an agricultural centre founded by the Romans. It has many fine buildings and among numerous churches a duòmo that is particularly noteworthy with an elegant, triple-arcaded tower and an intriguing Romanesque interior with della Robbia decorations — there are more terracottas from the della Robbia school on the façade of the *Ospedale del Ceppo*, a coloured frieze. The marble baptistery (designed by Pisano) is octagonal and particularly elegant. The son of the Pisano who carved the Pisa pulpit, Giovanni, provided a typical pulpit at S. Andrea with porphyrite columns mounted on stone lions. This church is a simple, very satisfying example of the Pisan Romanesque. There is a plain *pretorio*, and two rows of fine Gothic windows can be seen in the façade of the *palazzo comunale*, now housing the civic museum. Traditional and country recipes at **Il Boschetto** (0573-20185).

A road along the Valle di Brana with good views back towards Pistoia explores up to the Pass of Porretta (wide panorama) and so down to the edge of Emilia and the charming little spa of **PORETTA TERME** on the Reno. Return down the valley along the Reno and on through Prunetta to take 633 to the left in the direction of **MONTECATINI TERME**, and wind through the hills until you arrive at this most popular spa. Here there is a large park with thermal establishments and a funicular rail trip may be taken up to the old settlement of **MONTECATINI ALTO** on its hill with wonderful views. This is a good centre for walks. A detour west of the spa will take you to **PESCIA** (pop: 20,000) with a modern flower market and a 17th-century cathedral, and on to the village of **COLLODI**, birthplace of the author of *Pinocchio*. There is a monument and a museum. Nearby is the Villa Garzoni on a hill overlooking a lake: its 17th-century gardens are open daily. Roads north from here will take you up into the mountains as far as ski resorts, such as **ABETONE** with its ski and chair lifts — it is one of the best resorts for winter sports in the Apennines but is also good for summer activities.

West of Montecatini is **BUGGIANO CASTELLO**, with a church on its hill and other good buildings.

Here the road goes west to **LUCCA** (pop: 95,000), very rich in architecture and retaining its walls complete with 17th-century ramparts — you can walk around the circuit of the town looking over the tight maze of streets. The churches are particularly splendid with detailed and lively arcading and sculpture. The market occupies the site of the Roman amphitheatre, a circle of ancient houses, and some of the tall towers of the rival families exist from the 14th century. Lucca is famed for its excellent olive oil.

Return towards Montecatini and turn south into the wide valley of the Arno arriving at Fucecchio and then crossing the river and the autostrada to **SAN MINIATO** with its ruined Rocca (one of the remaining two towers is the belltower of the cathedral) and a bishop's palace; the birthplace of countess Matilda, the town was damaged by bombs in World War II, with the duòmo suffering badly. There is a museum beside the cathedral with religious pictures. Drive north to **EMPOLI**, also badly damaged in the war, and largely rebuilt. There is a good façade (part imitation) of Tuscan-Romanesque style on the Collegiata S. Andrea, and a museum of pictures. A good detour from Empoli is to the north on country roads through low hills to the village of **VINCI**, the birthplace of that greatest of painters, Leonardo. There is a small and fascinating museum in the old castello, with examples of his incredible machines (models) and drawings (reproductions) and a library. The *Museo Vinciano* is open every day; you will need to go to the nearby hamlet of **ANCHIANO** to see the birthplace (rebuilt). The road goes on from Empoli across the slopes of Monte Albano following the Arno to **LASTRA A SIGNA**, where you will find 14th-century walls and a fine *loggia* with polychrome panels. Cross the Arno to **SIGNA** where souvenirs on sale include straw hats and terracotta work. Drive on the Prato road towards the town of **CAMPO BISENZIO** where the front of the *palazzo comunale* has coats of arms of the captains and a fresco. There is a ruined castle. The route crosses the autostrada A11 to Lucca and enters Prato.

8 ABRUZZO

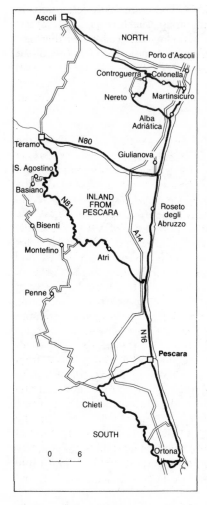

This is Italy often unseen by travellers who plod the familiar territory of the tourist sights. Close to Rome and easily accessible, the Abruzzo has no fabled Florence or busy Milan to draw the crowds although along its sandy Adriatic rim are many beach resorts facing the milky blue sea. The region is mountainous and roads curl and snake, inviting a slow discovery of rural pleasures. The food is often simple and the wines deserve to be better known; visits to *cantinas*, plain and functional though they are, are well recommended. There are sizeable towns — L'Aquila is the seat of the province and from its high perch you can see the Gran Sasso d'Italia mountains, swathed in snow — but also many small and beautiful places, often sited in high near-impregnable spots, and usually offering at least one good restaurant and a place to stay. The region is cut through with autoroutes so you can plan a quick arrival and then allow lots of time to negotiate your way. History is ever-present and nature so close that even avid hunters cannot kill it all off — one of the oldest wildlife preserves is the National Park in the south-west corner. The people cling to their roots, but even man cannot mar the scenic splendours of this wild region.

'Eleanora Duse wasted her talent and came close to smothering her genius when acting in the plays of Gabriel d'Annunzio,' observed Pirandello. Fortunately Pescara's bard was better at poetry, and that lives on . . .

PESCARA (pop: 122,000) has been relentlessly bombarded in the past and not much remains of anything prior to this century. Still, it is a modern city of wide streets and fine shops and you could do worse than use one of its many beach-side hotels as a place to stay, and spending an afternoon walking and visiting d'Annunzio's house (now a museum) near the Piazza Garibaldi. The **Carlton Hotel** (085-26373), right on the sea front, offers good rooms with sea views. There are many restaurants in Pescara and local specialities include roast suckling pig, fish broth, macaroni *alla chitara*, various sweets including the well-known Parrozzo which, still on the subject of Pescara's most famous son, was one of the poet's favourite *dolce*.

Inland from Pescara
1 day/140km

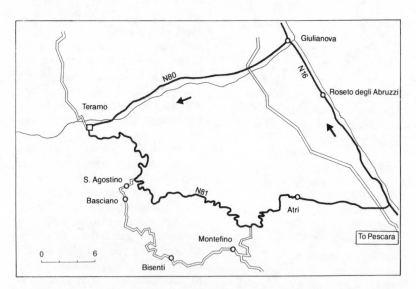

Pescara, the capital of its province, is a port and its suburbs straddle the coast so that as you leave on the main N16 you seem to go from town to town without a break, although there are large sea-facing gardens and sometimes pretty late 19th-century villas beyond the exotic greenery. Pines are the principal tree, however, and at Pineto, which is a little beyond our turning-off point, there are ranks of them. You will also see street vendors selling chestnuts — often very reasonable — and the nut is

Peak of Gran Sasso mountains

also used for cooking and sweets. Take the 553 left just before Pineto and duck under the autostrada at Silvi, yet another bathing beach — the *spiaggi* are flat and sandy and safe for children here.

Turning inland the road at once becomes hilly, and on either side are fields with olive trees so ancient they seem like old women crouched close to the soil. Here you begin to see sudden hills, often town-topped, while in the distance every so often gleam the heights of the Gran Sasso mountains, sugar pink in the sunset, a majestic sight. The road wriggles up the mountainsides as it approaches the towers of a hill-town, one of the most fascinating in Italy.

ATRI is one of the ancient towns of the region, with Roman origins well displayed in the centre of the narrow little settlement; under thick glass in the main piazza are mosaic pavements below the surface of the street, and others can be seen, including a lively dolphin, in the *cattedrale dell'Assunta*. This is the gem of Atri, a mainly Romanesque building which has been left much as it was built (on an earlier church in 1285). It has the rectangular façade unique to the Abruzzo and a campanile 55m high which soars over the town. Inside, bulky brick supports buttress the original pillars — look for the font with its Romanesque lions and elegant Renaissance cover of 1503. The town itself is lively and friendly with cafés and small shops, a pleasing mixture of styles from 19th-century balconied houses to the splendidly over-decorated Sant Agostino with its well preserved Gothic sculpture of foliage and faces.

Descending from Atri you might glance back to see if you can see the sun glinting from the polished plaques on the octagon-topped tower. The road continues steeply along to Bozza, where you take a right turn on the 81 towards San Agostino Basciano. This road offers wide-ranging views. [If you have plenty of time you might care to backtrack along the 81 towards **PENNE**, a fine medieval hill-town with beautiful views to the sea and also to the Gran Sasso range, from its 442m perch. There are several churches with not a few minor treasures.] The roads are good, but of necessity narrow and winding as you head towards Basciano where you might wish to take an alternative route to the 81, the 365 going through such pretty settlements as **MONTEFINO** with its view over the valley of the river Fino and its romantic chunk of a castle, once owned by the Aquaviva family, and **BISENTI** with a fine medieval tower and ancient fountains. Here also is one of those vast Baroque churches where you can see one of the local arts — majolica plaques usually in Baroque shapes and containing highly coloured views or religious subjects, usually framed with typical representations from the 18th century of garlands of flowers and leaves. The road winds on in sharp curves until it rejoins the 81 below **SANT' AGOSTINO BASCIANO**. Here there is a cheerful little piazza, a clocktower with steps leading up to its open archway, and typical layers of flat red roofs with wide sweeps of countryside beyond. A simple unprepossessing place, for a coffee perhaps, before continuing on the 81.

TERAMO is a comfortable country town at the junction of two rivers, the chief city of the province, with the imposing presence of a grand red brick cathedral standing guard. The duòmo was constructed in the 12th century, later enlarged with a square campanile — look for the impressive 14th-century doorway with its mosaic frame. There is also a fragment, not large but impressively solid, of a Roman theatre on the Via Teatro Antico, and other Roman remains can be seen in the town. There is a fine restored cloister to be seen at the Convent of San Giovanni.

After your exploration of the city a good direct road, 80, will take you along the valley of the Tordino river to Giulianova's beach. Here, you can choose to hurry south along the autostrada or turn right down the 16 towards Pescara. The road is a wide one and the flatness comes as a relief after the dippy mountain tracks! The little town of **GIULIANOVA**, just up from its *spiaggia* or lido, is worth a stop for here you will find an unusual circular church with a six-sided Renaissance exterior. The 16 hugs the sea, usually offering placid views and wide skies. You pass by the tiny church of Santa Maria a Mare, in fields of cabbages and corn; a fascinating little Romanesque building with a sculpted semicircular arched entrance. The straggling modern village of **ROSETO DEGLI ABRUZZI** has a fine soft sand beach and several places to stay, yet its main attraction must be the fine mountain views behind the town, with many villages on the hilltops.

It's now a short drive on to Pescara and dinner in town.

North from Pescara

1 day/about 170km

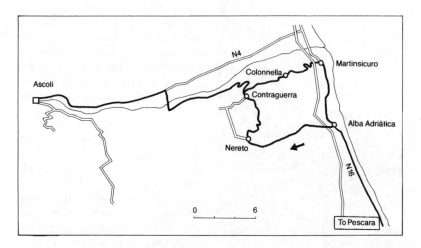

Leave Pescara on the same road north as in the first route following N16 along the coast — or if you wish to avoid ground already covered turn off at Citta St Angelo and take the autoroute north to Ancona (A14 marked with green arrows for Ancona direction). Beyond Giulianova route 16 continues to hug the sea, passing small beach towns and crossing rivers, with views over green hills. Before arriving at the river Tronto (border with the Marches) turn left along a small road branching from Alba Adriatico, following it under the autoroute towards the little town of **NERETO**. Here, above the river, take a pause and enjoy the superb views over the valley of the Vibrata towards the snows of the Gran Sasso; the morning light offers particularly fine glittering aspects. The roads are narrow, so you will have to proceed slowly, giving a chance to look at the vine terraces and the small irrigation ponds — there is actually little rain here and it has to be conserved.

Follow the narrow route from here to **CONTRAGUERRA**. Here can be seen a tiny Italian hill-town with a fine terrace and a tight web of streets — the Vicolo della Sciliana, the Vicolo non plus Ultra, neatly marked on blue tiled signs affixed to the houses — surrounding a minute piazza. A fountain plays against hillsides vibrant with colour, especially in the autumn when the vines are all copper and red leaves on their well-ordered terraces. Take time to visit the *cantina* of the Illuminati family and try one of the delicious, fresh wines. You may usually visit without appointment but to be sure write ahead to Azienda Vitivinicola (Dino Illuminati, 64010, Contraguerra, Teramo; 0861-856631).

Vines are grown all over the region, from the harsh hillsides to the coastal plains, and the wines produced are red, white and a distinctive local wine called after its lucid colouring, *cerasuolo*, and actually sometimes having a suggestion of a cherry taste. The white, *trebbiano*

Preparing grapes for wine-making

d'Abruzzo, is pale and very light in taste, while the red, *montepulciano d'Abruzzo*, is hearty and full. Many wines carry the DOC appellation as a guarantee of high standards and traditional wine-making, and you can always purchase wines at the *cantinas*, either in single bottles or dozens, or in mixed cases; but beware if you are flying home of buying too many bottles — they are not only heavy, but very often airlines will not carry boxes of wine as cargo and you will have to drag them on board with you. Check customs allowances before you leave — they are surprisingly generous if you buy outside duty free shops and have no other alcohol to take with you.

Follow the tiny road north and east to **COLONNELLA**, a typical hill-town sprawling over a height with views to the river and vineyards. Here you can eat well at the **Hotel Bellavista** (Via Icona 1; 0861-70132), a modern place with rooms offering fine views beyond a garden. The food is very much of local origin — rabbit, pancakes stuffed with different fillings, game, locally made pasta, cheeses and rich desserts. The terrace of the Bellavista offers a chance to sit and enjoy your espresso while looking out to the mountains — the large buildings of the local *cantina* are obvious. The Cantina Sociale Colonnella is big, bare and modern and it can be found in the midst of fields on the outskirts of the town at Ctr. Vibrata 43; 0861-77777. Visitors are welcome and the wines besides the red Montepulciano are Valvibrata Giardino and Valvibrata Sansavino (white). Either of the last two would be ideal for a picnic in this enchanting countryside, and bread, ham and the local *peccorino* cheese would make very good accompaniments to such a feast.

To continue you can either follow the winding road back to the coast at Martinsicuro, a small seaside resort, then turn left on the N16 and after crossing the bridge over the river Tronto follow signs for Ascoli Piceno along the N4; or you can descend from Colonnella by local roads and cross at one of several bridges joining the N4 farther along. This is a good, serviceable road with valley views somewhat marred by the presence of the autostrada across the river, although very often the Italian engineering genius can surprise with well-designed bridges and even enormous, valley-hopping 'flyovers'.

After 28km from the coast you come to the capital of the province, **ASCOLI PICENO**. This little city (pop: 45,000) is host, each 4-5 August, to one of these typically Italian events, the Quintania, which involves a parade of a thousand locals headed by the town worthies, all in 15th-century dress. The festivities conclude with a tournament and everyone enjoys themselves. There are fine buildings in the town so consider a leisurely walk to the duòmo (15th century), the charming early baptistery, the Roman gates and the *palazzo comunale* which includes an art gallery open to the public. There are several noteworthy churches — particularly S. Francesco — in a variety of architectural styles. Over the Tronto is a single arched bridge dating from Roman times, the Solesta Bridge, and there are a few scattered remnants of a Roman theatre. Around the Via Soderini in the town centre are many medieval houses and looming towers, and to see town planning as it was conceived 400 years ago, take a turn around the Piazza del Popolo which is screened with archways, a handsome sight with its statues and the ancient towered Palazzo del Popolo where the archaeological museum is lodged. Look for the courtyard here, an elegant Renaissance design. Ascoli repays a longer visit and there are good restaurants and cafés serving local specialities.

You can explore farther into the Marches towards Umbria, but this would entail a drive of at least two days since the roads are hilly and progress often slow, especially in inclement weather. Note the following towns as interesting excursions: **AMANDOLA** above Ascoli on the N78 in a handsome setting in the Sibillini Hills; on the N4 towards Rieti there is the small spa town of **ACQUASANTA** with sulphur baths and treatments, attractive hill views; **AMATRICE**, just off the N4 on the lake of Scandarella, a small high-placed settlement with good views and a notable church, in a lively pink stone. There are several winter-sports centres here for ski enthusiasts — **ANTRODOCO**, farther along the N4 at its junction with the N17, is in the midst of mountains, commanding some spectacular scenery. It is also a sulphur spa. Here you could continue back to Pescara via **L'AQUILA**. This city (pop: 60,000) is the capital of the Abruzzi and has many monuments. It would also make a very good centre for exploring the region.

If you are leaving Ascoli to go directly back to Pescara after a day out, you could go on the autostrada all the way, or meander through the northern parts of the region following the N81 all the way to Chieti, which is close to Pescara. If you follow this idea (which will present a variety of hill and valley scenery as you head down via Teramo and Penne) allow lots of time and perhaps a stopover on the route; but it is indeed much more rewarding than pursuing speeding lemmings down the toll-roads. An additional alternative is to retrace your route on the direct and well-kept N4 and N16.

South from Pescara

Half day/80km

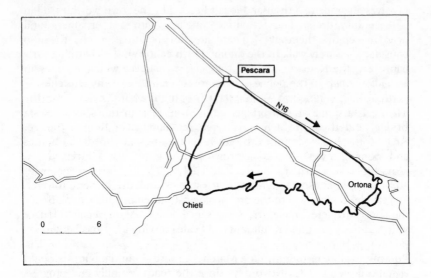

Leave Pescara on the N16 heading south towards Ortona. The road skirts the sea and is built up almost solidly for some distance with villas and small shopping centres. You pass through one of the many small bathing beaches along this coast at **FRANCAVILLA AL MARE**, which has an attractive aspect and good shops. Shortly after crossing the Foro river look for Stazione di Tollo if you do not wish to continue the 10km more into **ORTONA**. (The direction here is right for Miglianico.) The resort of Ortona stands on a promontory and enjoys fine views over the Adriatic, particularly from the viewpoint beside the castle. Leave the N16 following signs to the left into Ortona. The cathedral here has been much rebuilt and it is a tribute to the tenacity of the inhabitants that they rebuilt it from a heap of ruins after World War II bombardments. Fortunately, there are some elements of the early Gothic building to admire including a handsome doorway. Like Pescara, not much of Ortona escaped the bombs, but the 15th-century castle survives above the harbour, and there are pleasant seaside walks.

Continue along the narrow and busy N538 out of Ortona and head towards the autostrada. Just before the road traverses it, turn sharp right up a winding road towards **TOLLO**, which you will quickly reach, passing through folded hills covered almost entirely with vines. Yes, this is wine country again, and if you stop at the Cantina Tollo, a large modern co-operative, you can taste the wines of this locality — very good and worth considering for purchase are the Rocca Ventoasas — named after the perch of the white-towered church on its rock above the community. There are the *montepulciano*, *trebbiano* and *cerasuolo* selections, but other more full-bodied *montepulciano* reds are available. Don't be put off by the very modern aspect of this *cantina* with its rows of bald-looking metal containers — they still make the wine using oak casks as you will see if you take a tour (Viale Garibaldi, 66010 Tollo (CH); 0871-959726).

The scenery is very much bucolic views here, marred only by the occasional hideous new concrete villa, yet these will presumably soon be masked in the kindly embraces of creeper and palm tree, if not by the vines themselves. Olive trees are mingled in the terraces of vines, and the view every so often shows the autostrada, a not unattractive concrete snake swooping along by the sea. About 5km away along a narrow twisting road you will come to **MIGLIANICO**, where there is another wine *cantina* — this one has a large shop for sales. This is also a *cantina sociale*, meaning that it uses the grapes grown by local farmers — in this case a gathering of 600 smallholders, founded in 1960. Visits are welcomed (Via S. Giacomo, Miglianico (CH); 0871-95262). The views over the valley here are splendid, with a typical Italian townscape spread over the col of the cultivated hills.

Follow the winding road west towards Ripa, with signs for **CHIETI** (pop: 43,000). This important town sprawls along the valley of the Pescara river, and it is a town of considerable antiquity. The cathedral has unfortunately been much rebuilt, but it has a medieval belltower. Via Priscilla leads to a square where there are three temples, and Roman remains from Chieti's past can be seen at the museum in the park with an emphasis on sculpture and mosaics from the first centuries. There are fine views from the park, and a farther example of Roman architecture in the ruins of a theatre.

The route back to Pescara is well indicated and the N5 will take you along the valley of the Pescara back to the city, passing under the south-bound autostrada and taking you directly to the sea-front.

9 LATIUM — THE ROMAN COUNTRYSIDE
(Lazio)

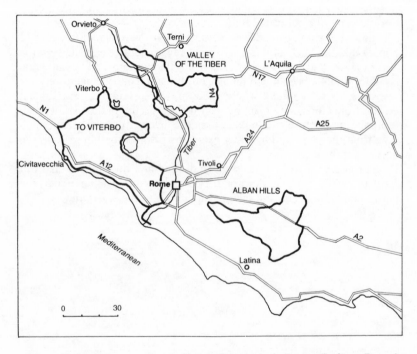

Although the Latium is centred on Italy's capital, Rome (Italian: Roma), it is a city that is becomingly increasingly difficult to drive in, so much so that legislation in 1987 promised rigid control and exclusion of many cars. My suggestion is to stay in a nearby town such as Ostia and take the fast and frequent subway system in to explore the centre, or other cities beyond the urban sprawl with their excellent train systems. Such a one is Frascati, on the slope of the Alban Hills, but there are many possibilities. Too many people converge on the Eternal City and see only Rome — if you can find time there is so much else just beyond the borders of the city. The *campagna*, the countryside of the city, is a large area of uncertain borders extending from the flat lands along the Tyrrhenian Sea to ranges of inland hills. Now the *Campania Romana* (Latin original, coined at the time of Constantine) is considered to include the irregular, uneven plain between the sea-marge and the Alban and Sabatini ranges of hills. The *campagna* does not include all of the Lazio (the modern name of the region) but in its loosest sense may extend beyond the region of the province of Rome. The Lazio has three other provinces and parts of these are explored in the three routes around Rome.

South from Rome: Alban Hills

1 day/170km/from Frascati

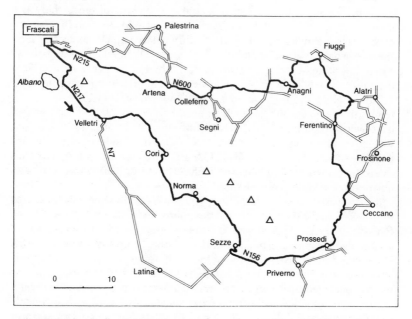

FRASCATI (pop: 20,000) is a holiday resort noted for its excellent white wine and for its sumptuous villas. Note particularly the Villa Aldobrandi with its gardens and fine views and, also in the town, the Villa Torlonia with a park and impressive array of fountains. Much of the town was damaged and destroyed in World War II and has had to be painstakingly reconstructed. There are several good churches and a castle, seat of the cardinal-bishop. In Piazza Roma are cafés and shops: the nearby Piazza San Pietro has been cleverly rebuilt, including the cathedral with its late Baroque front. There is a range of restaurants and hotels.

From Frascati there are several possible excursions, to other small towns known as the *Castelli Romani*, as well as to other villas. Our route takes us out of the town and towards **GROTTAFERRATA**, a quieter town cloaked with vineyards — the wine of the Castelli may be sampled

105

here. The most famous building is the abbey, which actually appears almost like a castle with its walls and moats. This was done by order of a cardinal (later Pope Julius II), and no doubt he had good reason. The monastery is found beyond the entrance court with its statue of St Nilo, who founded the abbey in the early 11th century. The establishment is a monastery of monks of the Basilian Order who officiate according to the Greek rite — they have beards and curious headdresses. Services are held in the church of Sta Maria in another courtyard. It is a most remarkable little building with fine marble carvings and an ancient door of wood, almost 1,000 years old. In the chapel of St Nilo, to the right, there are frescoes showing the saint's life. Another chapel, dating to Roman times, is thought to have given the town its name — it is called the *Crypta ferrata*.

From Grottaferrata, 215 runs east and at a short distance there is a turn to the left for the ancient city of **TUSCULUM**, beyond the gardens of the Villa Rufinella with its 16th-century palace. Thick woods surround the site which is at a height of 600m and well supplied with parking. There is a ruined theatre, a forum and, on the hill, an acropolis as well as the ruins of a medieval citadel. The views are impressive and extend as far as Rome. Here also is the famous *Tusculanum*, or villa of Cicero, and the remnants of an amphitheatre which once held up to 3,000 spectators and is known as the School of Cicero. Continue on 215 after retracing your way down the hill heading towards Colleferro. A side road to the left heading in the direction of **ROCCA PRIORA** brings you first to this interesting town on a height (the highest of the *castelli*) with good views down into the valley and the hills.

[If you wish to extend the route, you could continue on this little road to pass Carchitti and cross the autostrada following signs for **PALESTRINA.** This town, on the slopes of Monte Ginestro, is remarkable for a great Roman monument, the Temple of Fortune, which once spread over the whole area of the medieval town. Much was exposed after the removal of bombed buildings at the end of the war, and the temple occupied space from an even earlier temple when it was built 2,000 years ago. It can be seen from some distance, since the temple stands above the buildings of the town. At the top of the series of terraces and steps is the 17th-century Barberini Palace which was built over the remains of a temple which is conserved within. The palace houses the Museo Nazionale Archeologico Prenestino, containing local antiquities giving an idea of life in ancient Praeneste (Palestrina).

The town itself is interesting with narrow streets, often stepped, and there are remains of ancient town walls. The Piazza Santa Maria degli Angeli is on the site of the ancient Roman forum and at the same place is a monument to Pier Luigi da Palestrina (the composer's birthplace is nearby in the Vicolo Pierluigi), also the duòmo, a much-altered church founded in the 5th century and with a façade incorporating many ancient stones. The building is basically Romanesque, and it probably stands on an ancient temple to Jupiter. There are other remnants of the forum, including an unusual mosaic of a seascape and sections of Roman paving.

If you have all the time in the world, which perhaps you should in this area, go on to **CASTEL S. PIETRO** for the wide views — on the way there is a small church, Santa Rosalia, near to the Barberini Palace, which once housed a Michelangelo pietà, now in Florence. The Castel S. Pietro is actually a small village with a castle, and if you were to continue on this route across to Monte Tiburtini you will come to **TIVOLI** (pop: 42,000) with its famous fountains, water-cascades and gardens at the Villa d'Este. In Tivoli, a recommended place to eat is the **Cinque Statue** at Via Quintilio Varo 1 (0774-20366), reasonable with a cook-patron who supervises dishes. Tivoli's most famous monument has to be the **Villa of Hadrian**; a vast site, the most sumptuous and grandest of the imperial palaces, open daily (except Mon), much recommended as a special visit.]

Continue to the intersection of 600d at Artena and head towards Colleferro where you turn right just before the town to **SEGNI**. This is a very attractive small town — its name comes from *Signum*, a one-time settlement of the Volsces (in Shakespeare's *Coriolanus* the noble Roman general is pitted against the forces of the Volscians under Tullus Aufidius) — and there are walls dating from the 6th century BC, with two gates. Its acropolis is topped by a 13th-century church. Continue on a backroad, across the autostrada, to **ANAGNI**. This is a little town of much architectural distinction and it offers a fine panorama over the neighbouring hilly countryside from its terraces and Piazza Cavour. There is a 13th-century *palazzo comunale* and an earlier campanile to the cathedral which is part Romanesque, part Gothic with a 13th-century bishop's throne within. The town was the birthplace of no fewer than four popes, one notable one was Boniface VIII whose palace is near the cathedral. Restaurant — **Del Gallo**, via V. Emanuele (0775-727309).

Continue along the same road turning left at the crossroads and along a winding road towards **FIUGGI** situated at a high point and commanding extensive views. The little city is preceded on the road by **FIUGGI FONTE**, a spa set in wooded hills with two main thermal establishments for taking the water. The spa is popular in summer and often crowded. Take the road from here towards Fumone, passing close to the little Lake of Conterno. You pass beneath **FRASCHETTE** with its castle and then turn right for **FERENTINO**, once a Roman colony and known as Ferentinum. There is much to see including a particularly ancient town wall in part dating from the 6th century BC, and pierced with gateways. There are fine churches and the duòmo has a superb floor of mosaics of the 12th century (Cosmati) and antique columns. [From Ferentino there is a very attractive possibility of a visit to the falls of the river Liri where at **ISOLA DEL LIRI** the water tumbles in a series of descents — take the road towards Frosinone and follow minor roads through splendid scenery towards Sora. Return via the **Abbey of Casamari** on N214. If you admire the severe style of the Cistercian churches of Burgundy this is a must-see — austere and with windows still letting in a golden light through thin panes of alabaster. Try to ignore the canopy of the high altar — it's 18th-century exuberance would be all right in another church but here it looks merely vulgar in contrast to the elegant simplicity around. There is a shop where you can buy the monks' liqueur. Continue through the town of **FROSINONE** (pop: 30,000) which has a fine panorama of the surrounding hills from its piazza. Rejoin the main route at the point it joins N156.]

Continue south from Ferentino down to the valley through splendid scenery to cross the autostrada and arrive at Quattro Strade, where you take the right turn towards Ceccano and the junction with N156. Follow the sign for Prossedi, then head towards Priverno along the valley of the Amaseno — you can parallel the main road if you wish with rural roads crossing the river at Prossedi, perhaps going via the **Abbey of Fossanova** (more direct route from Priverno). This is another example of Cistercian architecture, even more celebrated than Casamari, in a beautiful position between the hills, still a functioning monastery and with many buildings to be explored beside the plain and satisfying abbey church. You can see the room where St Thomas Aquinas died and there is an extremely beautiful cloister. Return to **PRIVERNO**. This is a charming town with a fine *palazzo comunale*, neighbouring the vast shelf of the Pontine Marshes (the *Agro Pontino*) as does the next town, **SEZZE**. Placed high over the countryside on the edge of the Lepini range, this town was another Volscian stronghold and has remains of a temple and city walls. If you don't wish to climb the hairpin curves going up to Sezze, turn right and head towards **LATINA** in the plain. This modern city was built in this century on reclaimed marshland; it is the chief town of the province. Recommended restaurant is **Il Fioretto di Nilo e Nora** (0773-495273) a restaurant run by a family and with local dishes. You can rejoin the main route at Velletri crossing via Cisterna di Latina, a market town.

From high-perched Sezze continue along the western flank of the Lepini Hills towards Bassiano. Here look for signs to **SERMONETA**, once home of the Borgia pope Alexander VI who lived in its 13th-century castle. Towards Norma you will find an abbey very much influenced by Fossanova, **Valvisciolo**, with a handsome cloister. At **NORMA** is a curiosity — the abandoned town of **NORBA** reached on the way down to Doganella, a medieval settlement deserted because of fever. Ascend the winding road to Norma and leave the car for a walk to the ruins of Norba — this Volscian town still preserves its ancient walls. After Doganella continue towards **CORI**, an unusual two-part town with many ancient relics, up a valley to the right. There is a fine temple of Hercules with Doric columns and the remains of one to Castor and Pollux. Good views.

From here the road takes you across several valleys to **VELLETRI**. This was a Volscian stronghold and markets wines grown on the surrounding Alban Hills. There was much damage in 1944 from bombardments and the town has been reconstructed and rebuilt, but the restorations are very well done. Turn right off N7 on leaving the town (towards Rome) and follow 217 towards Frascati, passing on your way the Lakes of Nemi and Albano. Nemi is particularly beautiful, occupying an old volcanic crater and once known as the Mirror of Diana, with a wooded setting and its namesake perched beside it — **NEMI** is a pretty place with a castle. Turn right at the edge of Lake Albano towards **ROCCA DI PAPA,** one of the highest of the Castelli, with steep streets and good views over Lake Albano. The road beyond continues through Grottaferrata to your starting point at Frascati.

A good restaurant, and reasonably priced, is **Cacciani** (06-9420378) which has been in the same family for over three decades.

North from Rome: to Viterbo
1-2 days/250km/from Ostia

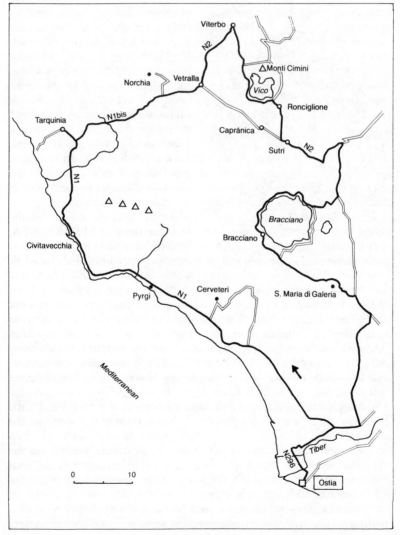

Rome — detail of fountain

As suggested at the beginning of the chapter, it is better to avoid Rome when driving, and a good alternative is the seaside resort of Ostia, which is connected by a direct Metropolitana service to the centre of the city, as well as by bus. In Rome (Italian: Roma) there are two main underground lines with a flat fare, and although spread out the city offers excellent walks. Indeed natives often say it is a city of villages. Take a good guide book (the **Blue Guide** is a good one, published by A. & C. Black, and frequently updated, while Michelin provides helpful gastronomic suggestions, as well as the *Guida Italia* published by Guide de l'Expresso in Milan, but in Italian). In Rome take good comfortable shoes and be prepared in summer for a great deal of heat; it is often wise to start early to try to get ahead of the inevitable crowds.

Mention **OSTIA** (pop: 20,000) and people think of the seaside resort, but that is actually the beach area of Ostia Lido, and old Ostia, often overlooked, is part of the settled area yet separate. It is a fortified village with about 3,500 people of the area's total, with a castle and several handsome restored residences inside the walls. The palace of the bishop, the museum in the castle, and the church of S. Aurea are the most notable buildings. Ancient Ostia is beyond this settlement, a vast site with many monuments and a museum, the Museo Ostiense, and it gives a rare glimpse into ordinary domestic life of the Empire — there are houses, shops, a well-preserved theatre and offices of the Roman guilds. In one bar, the Thermopolium, there is a counter and even places for hanging clothes! The excavations are set in a park, and Ostia Antica is well worth setting aside half a day to visit.

The resort itself is sometimes called Lido di Roma, which is correct since the beach is a very popular choice for Romans eager to get away from the city on hot days. (Out of season it can be quite uncrowded, but it is connected to Rome by a wide autostrade so access is very easy from the capital.) It is an extensive and increasingly extended resort, its apartments and hotels stretching along the seaside. There is a plenitude of places to eat. Just one: **Santa Barbara**, specialising in fish dishes and with a bar (06-5601327).

Leave Ostia Lido on 296 crossing the mouth of the Tiber and passing the airport of Fiumicino to the left. If you wish to hurry north take the E16 autostrada, otherwise the route follows the road which feeds into the N1 at Pte. Galleria in the direction of Civitavecchia. Across the flat shelf of land to the left, the Bonifica di Maccarese, are other resorts much quieter than Ostia Lido, such as **FREGENE**. On N1 drive north, stopping at **PALIDORO** for its ruins (once ancient Baebiana) and next **PALO**, beside the sea and possessing a Roman villa with mosaics and several very ancient tombs, as well as a 15th-century castle. Nearby is a pleasant resort, **LADISPOLI**, and just beyond examples of defence works such as the Torre Flavia. Continue along the road (this is the Via Aurelia) until a sign to the right indicates **CERVETERI**, a medieval town but situated in an area rich in Etruscan tombs.

[This makes a fascinating detour, since it was the old Caere, one of the major cities of the Etruscan league, and during the fall of the Roman Empire gave sanctuary to the Vestal Virgins when Rome was in the hands of the Gauls. Deserted due to malaria, it was re-inhabited and refortified; the walls still exist as does the castle of the Orsini, later altered for the Ruspoli family, standing on a pleasant piazza. The Etruscan necropolis is a site that can take hours to visit, depending on your interest in these fascinating and still little understood people. There are literally thousands of burial chambers, the most significant are open and reveal intriguing architectural design as well as paintings showing something of the life of the Etruscans buried here from 7th to 1st centuries BC. The necropolis is extensive, within a well-laid-out park, and it is wise to take some form of battery operated light since not all tombs are illuminated. From Cerveteri you can continue the detour up into the hills turning right to visit **CERI**, a town founded by the people of Caere fleeing the fever. It has a castle, but is now little more than a hamlet. Return down to rejoin N1.]

The Via Aurelia comes closer to the sea and continues to parallel the autostrada. At **PYRGI** an ancient port for Cerveteri was located — some of the port buildings can be seen underwater. There is a castle with a large round tower, built over Etruscan temples and an earlier fortress. In the temples inscriptions in Etruscan and Phoenician were found on gold sheets recording their dedication. Most of the area is now occupied by the modern beach resort of **SANTA SEVERA**. The mountains to the right are the peaks of the Tolfa range. The road passes **SANTA MARINELLA**, a pleasant beach resort also located on ancient foundations — this time Roman, but there are also Etruscan sites close by. There is a 16th-century castle. Continue along the coast into **CIVITAVECCHIA** (pop: 50,000), the modern port for Rome and point of departure for the ferries to Sardinia. It is an industrial city, hard hit during the war when much of it was destroyed, hence most of the buildings are new although the original port dates from the time of the Emperor Trajan and there is an Archaeological Museum in Largo Plebiscito. On the harbour is an impressive fort planned by Bramante and completed by Michelangelo who gave the fortress his name. Stendhal was consul here from 1831, and died here after completing an autobiographical work. Outside the town to the east are the ruins of Hadrian's baths, *Thermae Taurinae*. In Civitavecchia there is a bargain restaurant — **La Cambusa** (0776-23164) on the port with a verandah, fish specialities.

Continue on N1 north towards Tarquinia. The road bears inland after La Scaglia (Etruscan remains) and crosses wide valleys, one with the river Mignone coming down from the Tolfa Hills. Shortly after, turn right on 1 bis and follow signs for the city of **TARQUINIA** on its wide plateau from which there are fine panoramas of the local countryside and the sea. The city (pop: 15,000) has been somewhat spoiled by new development but its main interest, despite its picturesque medieval aspects with narrow streets around the church of S. Pancrazio, its squares and its towers, is the enormous Etruscan necropolis. This is the famous ancient Tarquinii, beyond the Porte Tarquinia on a neighbouring hill, and there are many intriguing remains of the city that was once the probable head of the Etruscan confederation. It is interesting as the site of the first archaeological explorations, commenced 500 years ago. In Tarquinia (it was called Corneto until earlier this century, a name it had held since its foundation in the Dark Ages) is the Museo Nazionale Tarquiniese, open throughout the year, closed Mondays, which contains many Etruscan remains.

The tombs in the necropolis can be grouped into four and require a good deal of time for proper viewing. They are intriguing not only for the wealth of detail they provide on Etruscan life, but also for their high quality of decoration dating from 6th to 2nd centuries BC. Bordering the necropolis site are parts of an aqueduct and at a distance is the acropolis with more remains. Return to Tarquinia and if you wish to make a short detour, drive down to Lido di Tarquinia, a resort with a beach. Otherwise, return to 1 bis and turn left across wide hills towards Vetralla. About 16km on, look for a small turn to the left towards **NORCHIA**. This is a small Etruscan site with tombs built like temples burrowed out of the volcanic tufa rocks, the temples with pediments and figures in relief. Return to the main road and continue to **VETRALLA**, a small town much damaged during the war but retaining its fine church, S. Francesco, and later frescoes within (followers of Gozzoli) and a stately 18th-century cathedral. Turn on to N2 towards Viterbo, passing through hilltop country with castles beside the rivers flowing west.

VITERBO (pop: 62,000) is a town that repays a long visit, but if you have only a short time park just outside this impressively walled town and walk to the centre. There are many fine medieval buildings, for Viterbo was once rival to Rome for the residence of the popes, starting with Leo Alexander IV. It is renowned for 'beautiful fountains ... beautiful women' and its symbol, the lion, can be seen everywhere. There are many fountains indeed, some very old such as the 12th-century one in the aptly named Piazza Fontana Grande. Even though attacked and damaged during the war, Viterbo maintains a medieval air and repays a long ramble with detailed guidebook in hand. Simon de Montfort's death at the battle of Evesham was avenged here in a church, the Gesu, by his sons who killed Prince Henry of Cornwall. In the Palazzo Papale the Viterbo popes were elected and at one famous election the cardinals were held prisoner until they elected a new pope — it took almost two years. On 3 September a procession carries a blazing device, called the *macchina di Santa Rosa*, to commemorate the saint's opposition to the seige of the Emperor Frederick II in 1243. The town is dark for this dramatic procession. There is a Romanesque cathedral, a great and very early campanile of S. Sisto, several other good churches and a Museo Civico to be noted, and the damaged Rocca and the ancient Via San Pelegrino should be seen; there is also a public garden without the walls at Porta Fiorentina. Try **Checcarello** for local food with a flourish at very reasonable prices (0761-28255).

Take the secondary road from Viterbo towards Vignanello, turning off almost at once towards **SAN MARTINO AL CIMINO**, up a road that passes through this high village with its views of Lago di Vico and 12th-century abbey. The mountain is an extinct volcano, farther to the north, and you can take a circular tour around Monte Cimino by going left towards the east, then north to **SORIANO** with its castle and road up the mountain (note also the fantastic fountain at Palazzo Chigi) and so around to the village of **BAGNAIA** with its grand and beautiful Renaissance palace, the Villa Lante, surrounded with a park and with a fine Lantini fountain. Return by completing the circular route around the mountain and heading back towards the eastern shore of the lake in the direction of Ronciglione. The main route continues along the other side of ·Lago di Vico for views across this stretch of water cupped in the crater of an ancient volcano. It was known to the Romans as Cininus Lacus.

The road takes you into the village of **RONCIGLIONE** which has medieval houses, striking church towers, a castle and a fountain of unicorns by Vignoli. The village looks over a gorge.

Ronciglione — town view

113

Beyond the village look for a turn to the right to N2 and **SUTRI**, once known as the Gate of Etruria and with some Etruscan remains. It stands on a rock and has a very well preserved theatre of 1st century BC, cut from the rock. In the duòmo are fine pavements, and one of the Etruscan tombs became first a temple and is now a frescoed church. North of Sutri is **CAPRANICA**, a high village where there are mineral springs, and the hospital has a Romanesque doorway. Drive south on N2 until a sign indicates **NEPI** to the left. This little detour takes you to a little town prettily placed between two *torrente*. There are charming buildings (a handsome *palazzo comunale* and a splendid Rocca as well as a cathedral with a Romanesque portico) and walls with a Roman gate. Outside, a necropolis has Etruscan tombs.

Return to N2 and continue to the intersection of roads at Sette Vene. [You can if you wish, follow the rivers down to the Tiber from Nepi, or join the next route which continues for about half its length from Civita Castellana to end in Rieti.] The road continues towards Lago di Bracciano through the hill slopes of Monti Sabatini. The lake is named after the Etruscan Sabate, and is another crater-lake, almost circular. The shores are wooded with olive trees. It is a beautiful drive around the lake: turn right to go through **TREVIGNANO ROMANO**, a pretty village with terraces and a ruined castle, probably the original Sabate. Pass the spa of Bagni di Vicarello and so into **BRACCIANO**, whose upper sections are towered and walled and contain a castle — the Castello degli Orsini which can be visited on conducted tours every Thursday and Saturday. It is a splendid example of a baronial home with its five great towers, well restored in the 19th century by the owners. Drive on along the Via Braccianese Claudia leaving the lake and taking the direction for Rome. If you wish to continue to drive right around the lake, turn left at the indication of **ANGUILLARA SABAZIA** which stands on a point above the lake and has a medieval castle: turn back along the road towards Sette Vene and take the Via Cassia towards Rome.

On 493 the route continues past Galeria to the right and a turning for the village of **SANTA MARIA DI GALERIA**, a picturesque place with a handsome gate and old houses; a walk will take you from a point below the piazza to the ruins of the castle on the site of an Etruscan settlement, Careiae. The main road joins the Rome road (N2) at the intersection of Madonna di Bracciano; continue to the circular road around Rome and turn right along this motorway until you see the signs indicating Ostia and follow the road the way you came, or else wait for the autostrada 8 bis which takes you directly into Ostia Lido.

The Valley of the Tiber
1 day/160km/from Rieti

This route is based on Rieti, which while not in the valley of the Tiber (Italian: *Tevere*), makes a very attractive stopping-over point in the deep

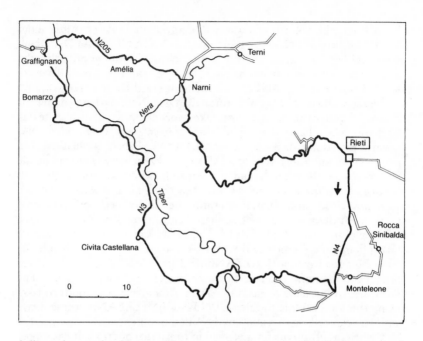

hills to the north of Rome. The route takes in some splendid scenery and for a while cuts into the territory of Umbria — a connection could be made with the route through Orvieto and on to Perugia if wished.

RIETI (pop: 45,000) is capital of a province and famous in classical times as the principal town of the Sabines. It is placed on the banks of the Velino and commands views over a fertile plain of Agro Reatino towards the Monti Reatini to the north. The wide boulevard to one side of the town shows the fortifications, a wall almost complete except for the break for the Piazza Mazzini. Here the church of S. Agostino has a good rose window and beyond is the Via Cintia with its 13th-century gate and arch of Vescovo of the same date. The Palazzo Vescovile has a fine loggia and an impressive great hall. There is a cathedral, much altered but with a fine Romanesque campanile and a later porch. In the Piazza Vittorio Emanuele, once the site of the forum, is the 18th-century *palazzo comunale* with a collection of sculpture. Beside the duòmo along the side of the Piazza Battisti are public gardens, offering good views. Rieti has connections with St Francis and there are several convents with associations in the neighbourhood, as well as a cave where the saint supposedly slept. There are several excursions that can be made from Rieti, notably up the mountain to see the panoramas. The ascent up Monte Terminello takes you to several winter-sports areas — there is a year-round funicular railway service. Rieti is served by an airport and regular train services. Restaurant — **Checco Calice d'Oro**, fairly expensive but with a fine atmosphere in its spacious room (0746-44271).

115

From Rieti take N4 south towards Rome, the Via Salaria. After about 10km turn left to make a detour up to **ROCCA SINIBALDA** where Torrente Turano swirls around a stately castle. Continue on down the steeply descending mountain road to pass through the village of **MONTELEONE SABINO** with a well-preserved church, 12th century and earlier. The route continues through Poggio Nativo where you have a choice of two roads — the first takes you along a parallel route via Castelnuouvo di Farfa, the second (reached from a little farther along N4) down a river valley takes you to **FARA IN SABINA**, a village with a grand view and the interesting **Abbey of Farfa** nearby, with mosaic pavements in the church and a campanile with frescoes of the 9th century. From these pleasant Sabine Hills come famous wines. The fine view down the Farfa valley is towards the Tiber, meandering in wide curves, and the road descends in sharp bends to a right turn and then a crossing of the river to **TORRITA TIBERINA** on the far bank, a castle on a hill in a sharp crook of the river. Another castle rears up beside the autostrada for Rome at **NAZZANO** and the route continues on across the hills to the right, heading for the village of S. Oreste and with views down the river valleys towards the Tiber. You arrive at 3 and turn right along the Via Flaminia towards **CIVITA CASTELLANA** where if you wish you can make a transition to the Viterbo route.

Civita Castellana sits on a plateau in romantic country, cut with steep ravines, crossed by high bridges. It has an impressive Rocca, a five-sided fort built for the pope Alexander VI, with dungeons and state-rooms of the Borgias. The duòmo is a splendid-appearing building with a portico by the famous Cosmati in the 13th century. There are mosaics around all three entrances and on the façade, but the interior was altered in the 18th century, although more mosaics on the floors and on a preserved part of the choir screen can be seen, and the crypt has antique columns. There are Etruscan remains in the vicinity — a temple and early tombs.

From here drive down the valley towards the Tiber along 3 — the route goes along the major river for some time giving views of its curving course. A road to the left will take you up to the castle of **Gallese**, but a most interesting visit can be made farther along where the road branches to the left at **ORTE** to leave the river for a time. Orte is also an Etruscan site and there is a museum of Sacred Art now housed in a church. Head for Bassano in Trevina and then take the turn right for **BOMARZO**. Here the Orsini family built a castle on a hill above the village and filled its large park with extraordinary sculptures in the 16th century. The *Parco dei Mostri* has enormous fantastical creatures, bizarre buildings and of course monsters, a veritable parade of the imagination, all settled in a suitably exotic garden. There is also a graceful temple by Vignola. Open daily.

Views to the left along 3 and 375 have given fine impressions of the bulk of the Monti Cimini. Now as the route proceeds north there are views in the distance of the heights around the Lake of Bolsena, which makes an attractive detour via the castle of **GRAFFIGNANO** all the way to **BOLSENA**, a one-time Etruscan town, on the volcanic Lake of

Bolsena, where the church is famed in Italy for a 13th-century miracle, giving rise to the feast of Corpus Domini, a major religious festival and a national holiday. There is a Roman theatre (superb views over the lake), catacombs and a castle — the upper part of the little town is medieval.

Continuing on the main route you now cross the Tiber and continue to the right on 205 after passing Alviano. With the river crossing we are now in Umbria, and connections can be made to the routes from Perugia via Orvieto or Todi. The road goes through wild green hills to **AMELIA** where there are spectacular walls around the little town, dating from 6–4 BC, composed of huge blocks of stone. The handsome campanile of the duòmo dates from 1050. Next town is **NARNI**, reached beside the ruined ponte d'Augusto which once carried the Via Flaminia over the river Nera. This ancient hill-town was the birthplace of Gattemelata, whose statue is preserved in Venice. There are some lovely buildings and a net of medieval streets to explore, a picture gallery, several fine churches and a 14th-century Rocca. **La Loggia** is a good and reasonably priced restaurant which serves local wines (0744-722744).

Beyond Narni take the road south along the hilltops towards Schifanoia and cross back into the Lazio at Santa Maria Maddalena. A lovely drive through the hills back to Rieti, with one suggested detour to the monastery of **GRECCIO**. It is at the edge of the plain on a high cliff, and was the original site of the mass of St Francis at Christmas when he invited in the ox and the ass. There is a Chapel of the Crib, with frescoes, to commemorate the origin of a Christmas tradition. The abbey was built here in 1260 and overlooks the Agro Rietino which we now descend to Via Terria and the road across the plain to arrive back at Rieti.

10 CAMPANIA AND MOLISE — THE NAPLES COUNTRYSIDE

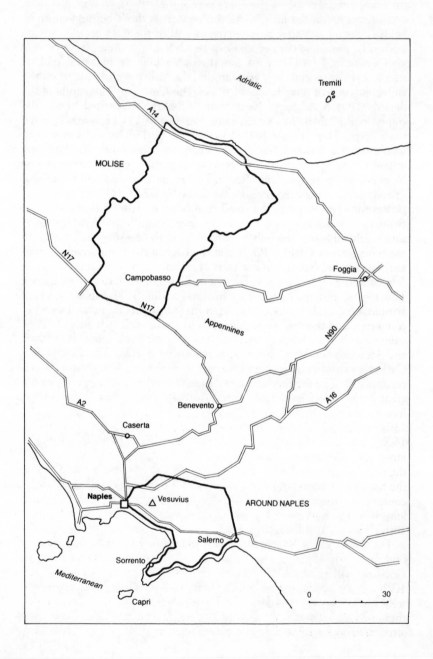

The Bay of Naples is rightly famous — and despite ravishments of pollution and overbuilding it remains a stunningly beautiful sight, its colour and sparkle unique. It has been beloved since antiquity, and many patrician Romans had villas nearby — life as the luxury-loving citizens lived it can still be experienced at sites such as Pompeii, where deluges of hot ash from Vesuvio's 1st-century eruption drowned the town 6m deep in cinder. The countryside around Naples is less pleasing now, cut across with roads and rail connections, decimated by poor planning and suffering from urban blight near the towns. It is hard to gain an impression of how this landscape once looked, yet as you drive along the Bay with its fabulous views you can still recapture past glory. Molise is not Naples country — but penetrate father to the east and you see more genuine countryside, especially as you enter Molise, one of Italy's poorest and simplest areas, with a farming population, yet with much to see for the traveller who doesn't want the conventional eye-popping Italian views. Molise's roads may be poor and its country plain, yet it is *real* Italy and the visitor who wants more than a dip into the Blue Grotto or a climb up glowering Vesuvio will find much pleasure here. Shepherds with flocks, crooked olive trees, stone temples and towers, and hamlets that seem almost glued to the landscape so tightly do they cling — these are the rewards of the traveller of today in the Molise and looked back on, they are often treasures indeed.

The sprawl of **NAPLES**, or Napoli (pop: 1,300,000) is a depressing prospect, but there is much to see and enjoy in this tight-packed city, the commercial centre and principal port of the south. There are excellent collections in the National Museum (many of the items found at Pompeii and Herculaneum) and many arts and sports events. The Teatro San Carlo is a world-known opera house, there is a music conservatory and a concert hall. The architecture varies from the sedate to the exotic, with a great flowering of baroque art especially in interiors, and the palaces often have imposing high gateways and outside staircases. Look for the 13th-century Castel Nuovo, the Royal Palace (*Palazzo Reale*, built in 1600), the towered Castel del Ovo on its island, many churches (one, S. Januarius, has catacombs which may be visited) and Capodimonte, where the royal palace now houses the National Gallery of Naples. You can tour the royal apartments here and then walk in the fine park with views of the country and the city — it is about 4km from the centre of town and the kilns where once the well-known Capodimonte porcelain was made in the 18th century can still be glimpsed.

For a stopover at Naples you have a wide choice of hotels but you may find the centrally placed ones noisy, so when booking ask about location. Good restaurants are **Al Poeta** (081-769 6936) and **Lo Scoglio** (081-808 1026) on the beach, simple and local yet well rated, and for an expensive treat **La Sagrestia** (081-664 186) is considered to be the best in town. But then in Naples you may be seduced into simply having pizzas — and here, after all, is where those delicious creations came from!

Around Naples

At least 1 day/about 160km/from Naples

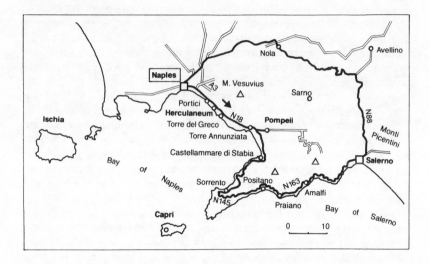

Take the road south-east from Naples towards Ercolano with Vesuvius towering blackly to the left. It is still an active volcano, and atop is a vast crater known as the *valle dell'Inferno*, wth the cone of the volcano at its centre. It is hard to believe that this inhospitable black ash eventually becomes very fertile soil. You can make a circuit by road, or by rail, ending in Sarno, and you can also climb to the top of Monte Somma, one of Vesuvio's peaks. The route goes along the edge of the sea through **PORTICI** where there is a *palazzo reale* of interest, even though the town is mainly industrial. Railway buffs will want to see the site of the first rail connection in Italy (1839; to Naples from here) and the national rail museum. Continue on to **Herculaneum** (Ercolano) for a visit to the excavations — the Roman city was deluged with rivers of mud in the 79 AD eruption and much was preserved to be discovered in the 18th century. The site is a neat and compact rectangle, and there are many things to see, notably domestic interiors and shops, some still preserving the items on sale when the catastrophe occurred. You will need a good deal of time to see the site properly, so (as with Pompeii) you may want to devote a whole day's visit. The road goes on to pass handsome villas with gardens and through the largely modern **TORRE DEL GRECO** (pop: 95,000). Here you can visit, if you are so inclined, the coral carving studios — there is also a museum on the subject. The fertile soil bears all sorts of lush plants here and Sorrento can be glimpsed across the Bay. Next comes **TORRE ANNUNZIATA** where there is a seaside resort and a popular spa. To the left a road goes to **Pompeii**, perhaps the most famous of ancient cities with the many buildings laid out along streets and around the Forum. Knowledge of the private and domestic life of the Romans is based largely on the findings here, and there is much to see in the spread-out town. There is a unique atmosphere, and a marvellous sense of history revealed as a living thing. Allow plenty of time for a visit. The modern village of the same name is a centre of pilgrimage at S. Maria del Rosario.

An island with a castle heralds **CASTELLAMMARE DI STABIA**, a resort and spa with many mineral springs. The original Roman town was also destroyed in the 79 eruption, and as with Torre there are remains of Roman villas to be viewed. There is a famous arsenal at the harbour and an ancient castle on a hill. The town is a centre for excursions into the peninsula of Monte Faito, walks offering wonderful views. Go on along the coast, close to the sea, to **VICO EQUENSE** with it Angevin castle and 14th-century cathedral. Finds from earlier settlements are on show at a museum. From here it is a short drive through Seiano and around the Punto di Scutolo for a fine view over the beautiful Sorrento plain. In the distance is Sorrento and beyond, the isle of Capri. The road traverses this lush plain with its citrus groves through **META**, a little village of charm standing above two tiny harbours, and other settlements before entering the gardens and villas of **SORRENTO** (pop: 16,000) on its high tufa terrace overhanging the sea.

This is a long, narrow town, tipped towards the blue of the bay, bright with flowers and scented with lemon and orange flowers in season. The

centre of the town is the Piazza Tasso, with a monument and views to the sea. There is a cathedral, an archaeological collection housed in the Terranova Museum at the end of the Via Correale, and several churches. There is a pretty 15th-century loggia, and some ancient stone doorways in the backstreets. Sorrento has very good shops and also makes an excellent centre for touring this part of Campania. You can go to little resorts such as Sant'Agata sui due Golfi and the Deserto, once a convent and with a fine view of Capri, or to **MASSA LUBRENSE**, with lovely views down to the sea. And of course you may go to **CAPRI** easily from here on small boats, either staying for the day, or exploring this pretty island with an overnight stay at one of its many small hotels. There is much to do, with excursions by boat into the Blue Grotto, drives up to the height of **ANACAPRI**

Sorrento

121

with the Villa San Michele, beautiful walks, and meals on the little piazza. For dining in Capri there are many good restaurants: try **Da Gemma** (081-837 0461), old, established and reasonable; or **Da Paolina** in a green garden, with excellent pasta (081-837 6102). In Sorrento you are also well served — note the highly rated **O' Parrucchiano** (081-878 1321), deemed the best on the coast.

From Sorrento cross the peninsula on the winding road to **POSITANO** to begin the wonderful drive along the Amalfi coast. You get a spectacular view from the Belvedere before entering this pretty little town with its brightly coloured arcaded houses and its beach. The church of S. Maria Assunta has a Byzantine painting. If you can tear yourself away from this spot, continue along the road towards Praiano. (Note that Positano has a festival in August with a sea-battle and fireworks.) **PRAIANO** is another pretty place, with a marina and wonderful views. Next comes the Vallone di Furore, a gorge, very steep and narrow. There is another grotto, named the Smeraldo, from the green colour of its lighting. You enter, as with the Blue Grotto, in a boat so allow at least an hour if you wish to visit. Cross the *Capo di Conca* and you will see **AMALFI** before you. High, white houses climb the hillside above a little harbour in this charming town, backed with tall cliffs, and with luxurious foliage. Amalfi has a Baroque duòmo and a cloister dating from an earlier construction, the Cloister of Paradise, started in 1266 and now a museum of architectural pieces. The town's maritime laws are enshrined in the *Tavole Amalfitane*, to be seen at the Municipio.

You can make a side trip up the Mulini Valley from Amalfi, or

Anacapri

122

continue on the coast towards Salerno. At **RAVELLO**, up the valley of the Dragone, you will find a superbly sited settlement with a fine cathedral. Originally Norman, it has been altered, but there are other Norman works in the town, notably the church of S. Giovanni, S. Maria a Gradillo and a fountain in a piazza. Notable too is the 11th-century Palazzo Rufolo with associations with the English pope, Nicholas Breakspear, and the Villa Cimbrone with marvellous views from its belvedere. A walk will take you to **SCALA**, a tiny settlement about ¾km away with a fine Romanesque doorway to its church. Drive on along the coast with its fine beaches and rocky wooded hills to Minori, and then to Maiori, both with beaches. If you wish to cut the rest of the route, take the winding road towards Tramonti with fine scenery until you reach the main Naples-Salerno road, along the curve of the hills from Maiori (or jump the main road and take the secondary one towards Pompeii). Otherwise our route continues to wriggle along the coast, with dramatic views of the sea and rocky ravines — stop if you can to enjoy the scenery which has often been altered by sudden floods from the mountains behind. Just before arriving at **CETARA**, a little fishing village of considerable charm, you begin to see Salerno across its bay. The elevated route now presents spectacular views until the bridge to **VIETRI SUL MARE**, a centre for ceramics as well as a beach resort.

SALERNO (pop: 160,000) is a town that has suffered from wars and also from the soil ruptures of 1954. In 1943 the American 5th Army landed south of the town, which was heavily bombarded at that time. The location of the town in the centre of its gulf (Paestanus Sinus to the Romans) is superb, with an old quarter shadowed with the castle of Arechi on the slopes; below is the modern town with a beach and a harbour. In the cathedral of S. Matteo are ancient columns beyond its Romanesque doorway and its bronze portals, cast in Contantinople in the 11th century. The interior is impressive with three aisles and fine mosaics, two 12-century ambos with a candelabrum. In the Chapel of the Crusaders soldiers came to have their arms blessed before sailing away. Pope Gregory VII is buried here, and the remains of S. Matthew are in the frescoed marble crypt. There is a museum with a striking ivory altar front of 54 panels dating from the early 12th century. The old quarter invites strolling — there are some good buildings of the Middle Ages, note the *Archi Arechi* of the 8th century and the shops and houses along the Via Mercanti. The Museo Provinciale contains ceramics (an industry of the town, along with the cultivation of spring vegetables) as well as archaeological items. There is a fine view from the already mentioned Lombard castle.

[A detour from Salerno can take you to the magnificent and romantic site of the city of **PAESTUM**, about 45km away. Here you should allow time from driving for a long saunter amidst these evocative Doric temples at the edge of the Sele plain. Besides the well preserved temples there is a long stretch of city wall. In the small yet excellent museum are *metopes* — 6th century, 33 in all — from the nearby sanctuary of Argive Hera at the mouth of the Sele river. Note also the rare murals from the Tomb of the Diver. The area has a marvellous atmosphere that must be experienced; a real sense of the lost grandeur of Greece.]

From Salerno take the parallel secondary road beside the main one towards Avellino, signed for Mercato S. Severino, where you continue on through the open high countryside with the wild Monti Picentini on your right. Turn left towards the village of Forimo and follow the road through pleasant scenery to **NOLA** (pop: 30,000), an ancient settlement, once Etruscan and later Roman, well known for its Greek vases in antiquity. Here, it is believed, church bells were invented by S. Paulinus, the bishop of the town in the 5th century. They are called in Italy *campane* from Campania. There is a celebration each 22 June. Nola has several fine buildings, notably a Renaissance palace of the Orsini, as well as that of the Covoni. The duòmo is neoclassical, rebuilt after a fire. The brave heretic, Giordano Bruno, burnt at the stake, was born here and there is a piazza named after him.

From here you can take the main road back to Naples north of Vesuvius, beside Monte Somma. Pass through Marigliano and Pomigliano d'Arco — just north is **ACERRA**, a city destroyed by Hannibal in the 3rd century BC. There are good mountain views, and nearby the deserted ruins of **Suessola**, destroyed in the 11th century. From here it is an easy drive into Naples. The port also has regular sailings to Capri, as well as Sorrento, and a visit to Ischia if you have time is also a good idea, with an additional boat trip once you have arrived, as a suggestion to see this beautiful, volcanic island with its mild climate encouraging a riot of vegetation. The tour around the island by sea gives many fine views of bays, beaches and cliffs.

Molise

1 day/230km/from Campobasso

The capital of this small region, **CAMPOBASSO** (pop: 45,000) is centrally located for a visit to Molise. The city is divided between plain and hill, with the old quarter on high as usual, and with a 16th century castle above, presenting fine views of the mountain and the town. Once cutlery-making was a major occupation; scissors are still made and the region still emphasizes that many small artisan shops can be found here, from copper items to pottery and saddles. The churches of S. Bartolomeo and S. Giorgio have good early sculpture and a new museum of antiquities of Samnite origin has been organised in the Palazzo Mazzarotta. There is a curious festival at Corpus Domini, when actors in metal supports present miraculous happenings as they are carried in procession. Recommended restaurants are **Il Potesta** (0874-61601) and the small and simple **Cecchino** (0874-64617), a bargain with traditional dishes.

From Campobasso go along 157 until its junction with 87, turn right, climbing in wide curves. Watch for the imposing S. Maria della Strada church to the left on a hill and at Campolieto you arrive at the watershed and start the descent of the Appennino Napoletano with wonderful views. The route goes right along the hills towards S. Martino in Pensilis where it joins 16 ter to the coast, but you may prefer a more direct way down the road to **LARINO** (87) where you will find an ancient town with a Gothic cathedral of the early 14th century and a later campanile. There is a stair studded with bits of Roman work at the *palazzo comunale*, and mosaics in the Library, as well as medieval sculptures. There is a good deal to see at the ancient site of Larinum (around the Piazza S. Lorenzo) with Roman ruins including a fine early amphitheatre. Each May (normally 25, 26 and 27) there are torchlight processions with ox-carts on the festival of S. Pardo. From Larino continue on the road down to the plain below and the town of Termoli. The route itself takes a longer way towards S. Croce di Magliano, a simple rural road, with a very good restaurant to be found at the already mentioned S. Martino — **Chez Nous**, a find, and well worth the long drive. Good wine, local food (0875-60752).

The road crosses to the coast past the autostrada to arrive at **TERMOLI**. This seaside town (pop: 20,000) has had a violent history of earthquake and war damage, notably during a Turkish battle in the 16th century. The town stands on a peninsula huddled in with its medieval walls, and gives a fine impression. There is a 13th-century castle and the cathedral is of the same date and possesses a good façade. There are mountains behind the town, and to the east rises the Gargano promontory. The tiny Tremiti islands can be reached directly from here by regular hydrofoil or ferry service. A good restaurant at the Hotel Corona is the **Bel Ami** (0875-3705) by the station, or the very good fish restaurant **Lo Squalo Blu**, which is highly rated and moderate in price (0875-83203).

A drive along the coast will take you to **VASTO**, the ancient Histonium. Just over the Abruzzo border this little town stands on a hill of olives above a good beach. A Gothic doorway in the cathedral and a 16th-century palazzo are worth seeing, and there are ruins of a 13th-century castle.

From Vasto, 86 bears directly inland, up past Cupello, climbing and then dipping down to inland valleys. Fine views from the heights. The road runs on to **AGNONE**, a holiday town on a hill — there is a charming church with a rose window. Beyond is the winter-sports resort (also summer), along a side road to the right, of **CAPRACOTTA**, impressively sited. Also nearby and to the left is the small and attractive settlement of **PIETRABBONDANTE**, high up and close to an ancient site — that of the Roman Bovianum Vetus. Here you can see a theatre and a temple, as well as remnants of a town wall, south of the village.

Join 85 and turn right to arrive at **ISERNIA**. This town is an ancient capital of the Samnite race, and easily spotted on its solitary hill, which must have been easy to fortify — its once important strategic position is underlined by the fact that it stands in the middle of the land mass at a crossroads. In the town there is a museum and fine impressive walls of polygonal stones. There are marvellous views all around from the town, in the east the Appennino Napoletano and to the south the Monti dei Matese. Follow the main N72 between the two mountain masses following signs for Benevento, turning off at **VINCHIATURO**, a pretty town of mainly modern buildings which was badly damaged in an earthquake in the early 19th century. [If you wish, detours can be made from here to explore the Matese, dramatic and little known mountains with valleys and steep cliffy gorges, heavily forested and still possessing considerable wildlife. It is a marvellous place for those who like the open air and near-untouched landscapes. From the village of **CERCEMAGGIORE** you can climb up the heights of Monte Saraceno, to view three regions from the top — not only Molise but also Apulia and Campania. There is a Samnite village nearby, with the remains of walls. A worthwhile detour could take you to **BENEVENTO**, where you will find Roman remains (a theatre and a fine Arch of Trajan) and a cathedral with a delicate campanile. There are several good restaurants — try **Vecchia America**, a place redolent with nostalgia for emigrants to the new country (0824-24394).]

From Vinchiaturo climb along a twisting ascending path with good views around the Monti di Sannio to arrive back at Campobasso, standing out with its six-towered castle of the Monforte as a landmark to welcome you back after a long tour of the simple yet splendid Molise.

11 APULIA (Puglia)

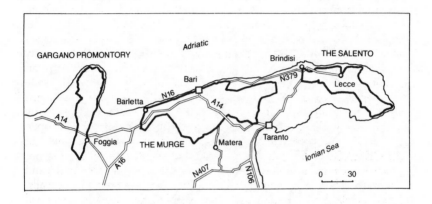

The heel of the Italian boot is a mysterious region. Closer to Yugoslavia
and Albania (across the Adriatic and the Straits of Otranto) than it is to
much of the rest of Italy, it had attracted colonists from much of Eastern
Europe. Its ports, principally the major one of Brindisi, have been
connection points between Rome and Greece for many centuries. The
Appian Way connected the area with the Roman Empire so it was always
vital for trade and indeed the whole region was a sort of bridge for the
ancient world. The roads and railways are well maintained today, for
Brindisi and Bari have important shipping connections as well as airports,
and even lesser ports such as Otranto and Manfredonia have important
ferry services. You will have little trouble finding your way around this
region, for in addition to being undulating it is also not crowded, and in
some parts centres of habitation are quite far apart and the scenery is wild
and seems almost untouched by the hand of man. It is a land ruled by the
sun: the long hot summers tend to parch the soil and not surprisingly,
much of the land, and the coastline in particular, will remind the frequent
traveller of Greece and Turkey. This is the fabled land of sun and sea that
many sybaritic voyagers will welcome; it also has a great deal to offer those
who are willing to explore the lesser roads and natural areas of the interior
— even though a glance at the map will show you that Apulia's border is
wrapped almost three quarters by the sea.

Apulia is connected by direct autostrade along the eastern coast and
across the peninsula from Naples. The railways descend from Ancona and

points north to service the region, and also from Naples and Sicily. There are airports at Bari and Brindisi with connections to Rome, so you don't have to drive all the way down to arrive at this ancient, strange and often oddly compelling part of Italy's south land with a character all its own.

The Salento
1 day/375km/from Brindisi

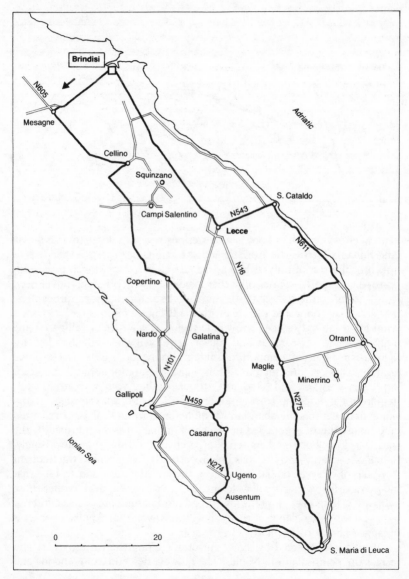

BRINDISI (pop: 90,000) has an excellent natural harbour from which boats depart to Greece and its islands (car ferries and hydrofoils). It is an ancient city, known to the Greeks, and was a Roman port by the 3rd century BC, becoming a navy base. It was important in the Crusades, but later declined, especially after a 15th-century earthquake. It regained importance after the opening of the Suez Canal and was notable for actions during both world wars. It is the capital of its province. The city is set on an apron of land between the arms of a landlocked harbour — on the Seno di Ponente is a large monument to the Italian navy which can be climbed (lift) for the view which takes in the whole harbour and the fortress of Sant'Andrea island. There are pleasing drives around the city; note the marble column at the top of a flight of steps off the Lungomare Regina Margherita — it marks the end of the Appian Way. The cathedral was originally ancient (there are animal mosaics around the altar) and is a plain 18th-century structure with statues of bishops along its roof. Medieval sculpture from the cathedral can be seen before the courtyard of the provincial archaeological museum (sculpture, ceramics, glass and coins). There are several good churches, notably S. Benedetto, 11th century, fine campanile and cloister, and the circular church of S. Giovanni al Sepulcro, also Romanesque and originally a baptistery. The 12th century Tancredi Fountain is on the Strada Statale Adriatica. There are good, simple hotels in the city centre, and a recommended restaurant is **Il Pescatore di Jaccato** (0831-24084) where fish is presented in a distinctive southern manner, as well as a 'Greek dinner' (needs ordering in advance).

Leave Brindisi and go towards Mesagne, but a detour can be made to the fine 14th-century church of S. Maria del Casale to see the frescoes and impressive polychrome façade — beside the airport. This 14th-century church obviously had connections with the Crusaders — see the fresco of the knights. Cross the N379 and continue along N7 (the Via Appia Antica) straight to the market town of **MESAGNE** (pop: 30,000). It has a Norman-built castle, later transformed to a Renaissance palace, in the old town. There is a museum, and a church with an ancient crypt, Chiesa Madre. Continue towards Lecce on 605, turning left at a small side-road after about 10km to **CELLINO S. MARCO** with a castle, and detours if you wish to **SAN PIETRO VERNOTICO** with the Roman ruins of Valesio (walls and part of the baths) and **SQUINZANO**. This little place has a delightful and ancient abbey with fine carving and frescoes. Next to the church is a folk museum. Both of these villages can be visited on the return route if you wish.

Continue along to cross 7 ter near Gagnano where the road goes to Lecce and go through **SALICE SALENTINO**, a centre for local wines. Head towards **VEGLIE** with its little church and a hotel. Continue on to Leverano and then turn left to **COPERTINO**. Here there can be seen a large castle with a moat, and a tall, French-style keep. The castle is well worth a visit, a whole mix of periods with the great rooms of the central Castello Vecchio. Drive on towards **GALATINA**. This is an important centre for wine and a stop is suggested to try the local product. Galatina was a Greek preserve in the medieval era. It is sited right in the midst of the Salentina, which the route has been passing through since crossing the provincial border just before N7, and the agricultural centre of Campo Salentino. This is a flattish plain never very high and with few hills except for the rock outcrops that dot the landscape. There is little unusual scenery in this part of Apulia except for the cliffs beside the sea, and these are often steep and dramatic, dropping down to the sea and forming grottoes below the surface of the azure water. If you wish to make a break for a meal in Galatina and take extra time to see the 14th-century church of S. Caterina d'Alessandria, (which is entirely covered in frescoes inside and has a handsome sculptured façade with a rose window), then try **La Capanna** (0836-64048), a local restaurant that still promises surprises, and reasonable. Other churches are Baroque, but it is the first one that underlines the power and prestige of the Orsini family who were lords here.

[Side trips can be made here to the west to see **NARDO** which possesses a triangular piazza and its houses have ornate ironwork balconies and loggias. Look for the church of S. Domenico with a parade of weird sculptures across its Baroque façade. There is a much altered cathedral that has suffered since an earthquake destroyed it, and the town hall is a building of the early 16th century with battlements. There are still fortifications and odd architectural conceits such as the Osanna. On the road from here is **GALATONE** with Baroque buildings, which is on the way to **GALLIPOLI** on the coast. This town with a famous ring to it (though it is not *the* Gallipoli), is antique and tightly packed on its peninsula jutting into the Ionian sea. There is a large and stern castle with huge corner bastions and a museum of antiquities. The duòmo is early 17th century and in another Baroque church, the Purita, the floor is all majolica tiles depicting flowers and fruits. Gallipoli is famous for the vinegar it produces.]

From Galatina continue south to **PARABITA** where there is a castle, and then veer right for **CASARANO** where there is an early church with mosaics in the vault and in the cupola. The Casaranello, as it is known, also has 13th-century frescoes. Head for the sea from here via Ugento and the ancient Roman harbour of Ausentum to the sea, where you turn left and drive along the Ionian shore towards Capo Santa Maria. The coast is indented with rocky bays and studded with ancient watch towers. Before long you will see the high cliff of Capo Santa Maria di Leuca, just beyond the most southerly point of Apulia at Punte Ristole. Bathing places and a lighthouse. There is also sailing and spearfishing as well as caves (excursions by boat). Go north from here on N275 towards Lecce. On a road to the left is **PATU**, where a building is claimed to be very ancient, the Centopietre, made of stone slabs. On the right **TRICASE** has a castle of the 16th century and an imposing 18th-century church.

The road skirts **MAGLIE**, but it is worth diverging to the left to visit the Baroque buildings of this town and a paleontological collection in the Palazzo Capece. Much of the material came from local caves.

You may go on to Lecce on N16 or take a coastal route via Martano to the right — in the latter case, on reaching **SAN CATALDO**, a beach resort with camp sites, take N543 for Lecce.

LECCE (pop: 90,000) is the largest town on the Salentine Peninsula and is a very important centre for Baroque art. Visit the Piazza Sant'Oronzio with its Roman column; the Roman amphitheatre nearby; the churches of Santa Croce, the duòmo with its tall campanile, the exotic Rosario and for a change from 17th-century tastes, Santi Nicola and Cataldo, a striking Norman Romanesque structure — though it has not escaped a florid Baroque façade. There is a fine Renaissance cloister. You should also see the Governor's Palace, the Palazzo Vescovile and the Seminario with its grand courtyard. The Provincial Museum at Palazzo Argento has a varied collection of archaeological items as well as pictures and ceramics. There are many other Baroque buildings to see and a good restaurant is **Il Satirello** (0832-656121).

From Lecce it is an easy drive on a straight road back to Brindisi, or you may detour via the remaining coast road north.

The Gargano Promontory

1 day/120km/from Foggia

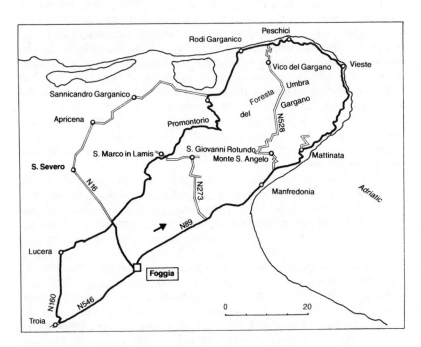

The Gargano is a knob of land at the northern end of Apulia, the spur on

131

the boot, thrusting out into the Adriatic Sea. It also happens to be a region of particularly interesting geological make-up, and out of the whole Gargano promontory few streams run to the sea — they vanish into the caves and grottoes beneath the thin soil of the mountainous limestone mass, for of all Apulia this is the only high part. The scenery is very fine, with steep hillsides descending to the clear blue of the sea, for most of this route is around the coastlines and frequent stops are suggested where possible to take in views that sailors of antiquity would have known well.

The base for this route is **FOGGIA**, although there is not much of interest in this modern town (pop: 150,000) apart from the duòmo which retains part of its 12th-century aspect; the rest was rebuilt in the 18th century. There is a museum with folk art and a modern picture gallery, as well as local archaeological finds. Much of the town was lost in an earthquake in 1931, and war damage took care of the rest. The public gardens are pleasing and there is a grand Baroque church in del Calvario with its cluster of chapels. Umberto Giordano, the composer, came from here: there is a monument in Piazza Giordano. There are several good restaurants — one at the **Hotel Cicolella** (0881-3890) and a good fish restaurant is **Nuova Bella Napoli** (0881-26188).

A straight modern road takes you right across to the sea and the port of **MANFREDONIA**, which would also make a good base for those wanting somewhere smaller and more atmospheric, for although it is an industrial town it faces the sea and has some monuments, notably the castle with its great bastions. It is now a museum of archaeology with material collected from the Gargano. From here ferries leave for the **Tremiti Islands**, making a fascinating trip although you will need more than a day — the ferry crossing stops at Vieste, Peschici and Rodi Garganico before crossing to the group of little isles, three in number and composed of limestone. They are popular with tourists for their climate and simple scenery. Hydrofoils now ply from several points although the service is limited in winter. If you stop in Manfredonia seek out S. Domenico to see its fine Gothic doorway and frescoes. **Al Gambero** is a recommended fish restaurant (0884-23255).

Geologically the Gargano is a part of Dalmatia, not Italy, and its steep sides rising to Monte Calvo are still wooded, principally with oaks. From Manfredonia take a road towards the skirting highway to the north and visit the ancient site of **Sipontum**, a settlement in pine woods. The town was deserted in the 13th century as local marshes became swampier and malaria probably hastened the demise of the town, although there was an earthquake in 1223 which destroyed most of the buildings, yet sparing the fine 12th-century church of Santa Maria di Seponto which can be visited. It has a simple, square plan with mosaic fragments and the whole has an Oriental sense. Beneath the church is a crypt with ancient columns. The front has a porch and a sculpted doorway. Nearby is a beach resort, the Lido di Seponto, just to the south-west of Manfredonia.

From Manfredonia take 89 onwards (our road skirts the entire peninsula) and follow the coast road, looking for signs for **MONTE SANT'ANGELO**. The road climbs in sharp hairpin turns to this little town high on its rock spur. The Sanctuary of St Michael should be visited, deep in its grotto. There are other noteworthy churches and a castle surmounts the town, now a massive ruin but worth the climb for the view. [You can cut across the promotory here if you wish, on 528, a mountain road, going through the Umbra Forest and down past Vico del Gargano towards the coast, rejoining the route near S. Menaio.] The road continues along the coast, ascending and arriving first at Mattinata, and continuing with many a curve and plenty of fine views, towards Vieste. [An alternative is to follow 89 across the end of the promontory and over a mountain pass — a difficult winding road through rocky terrain.] Our route, however, bears to the right at Mattinata to pass through the resort of Pugnochiuso and on to **VIESTE**, a little fishing village with a castle on a promontory. From here you can make an excursion to the Grotta Campagna, a high-ceilinged cave, by boat. Continue along the eastern edge of the Gargano to arrive at **PESCHICI**, a clifftop settlement near the cave of S. Nicola and the viewpoint of Monte Pucci with wide views of the coast. A little farther and a long beach can be seen at Menaio and you drive through ranks of olive and orange trees to the village of **RODI GARGANICO**. This attractive village on a point is a fruit-growing centre and there is a beach, as well as ferries for the Tremiti Islands.

The road starts inland with the Lago di Varano to the right. A direct route back via Sannicandro Garganico can be made with a stop perhaps at **APRICENA** to view the ruins of the castle. At **SAN SEVERO** join 16 for Foggia. Here there is a restaurant of medieval origins serving the light local white and rosé wines — **La Botte** (0882-22983).

The route crosses the promontory from Cagnano Varano towards **SAN MARCO IN LAMIS** along a mountain road — here is a convent, San Matteo, of somewhat forbidding aspect — it was originally Benedictine and important in the area. Not far off is the village of San Giovanni Rotondo below Monte Calvo, the highest point of the Gargano. **SAN GIOVANNI** has several interesting ecclesiastical buildings and is a centre for pilgrimage to the tomb of Father Pio. The hospital here is named after Fiorello La Guardia, an ebullient mayor of New York City. Our route continues down the edge of the Gargano hills and crosses the Tavoliere plain towards the autostrade A14, and beyond to 16, where we make a crossing to follow the directions to **LUCERA**. This is a town with much atmosphere and an impressive castle, built in the 13th century and containing earlier elements within its complete curtain walls and numerous towers. The duòmo is little altered from its 13th-century origins. It has a restrained façade and is a mixture of periods — mainly Romanesque and Gothic, yet with Roman pillars and a 16th-century addition to the tower — the apse has unmistakable Angevin elements. 18th-century palaces stand nearby and there is a pretty public garden and a museum with Roman, Saracen and Angevin works. Follow 160 south across valleys to **TROIA** with a remarkable cathedral of the

11th century in a fusion of disparate styles — Pisan Romanesque and Byzantine, principally. There is a sober façade with animal sculptures, fine rose window and 12th-century bronze doors. The interior is simple, yet with rich sculpture and an early pulpit. There are silver liturgical vessels and statues on show in the treasury. Nearby is another early church, S. Basilio, a domed building of the 11th century reflecting the Pisan style. From Troia the road, 546, goes straight back to Foggia.

The Murge

2 days/380km/from Bari

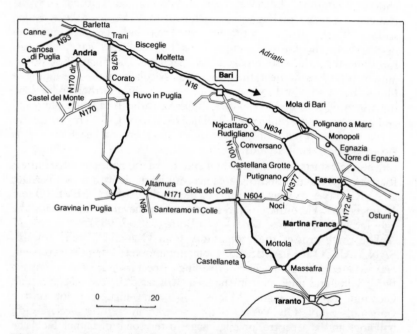

This route takes in the shore of Apulia with numerous small resorts, facing the waters of the Adriatic, to meander through. There is some breathtakingly beautiful maritime scenery and picturesque little villages, and it penetrates inland to explore the Murge limestone plateau and cross the upper heel of 'the boot' as far as Taranto if wished.

The suggested base here is **BARI**, the capital of Apulia, and with close to 400,000 inhabitants one of the biggest centres of southern Italy. It's a busy port with a fringe of oil refineries and is the passenger and freight centre for the Eastern Mediterranean. There are connections by sea to Greece and Yugoslavia, as well as Ancona up the Italian coast. It is a very ancient town, and has had many overlords from its Illyrian or Greek beginnings to Romans and Normans, and later Austrians and Bourbons.

Despite bombardments in the last war it maintains an intriguing maze of an old town — the *Citta Vecchia* on its promontory,, topped by the ancient shrine of S. Nicola and with the cathedral nearby. Most of the monuments are here, hotels are in the modern quarter beyond, the well-laid-out *Citta Nuova*. A walk around the old town is essential, even if you get lost! Look for the Castello with its moat (drained and now a garden) to see the inner courts with much sculpture and the Norman keep (may be visited). The cathedral is 12th century with a handsome façade and campanile and a *trulla*, a baptistery altered in the 17th century. Simple, impressive interior with a bishop's throne and a 12th century baldachin. S. Nicola, the only building in the city to survive the revenge of the Normans who levelled it in the 12th century, is the first church of its type in Apulia and provided the inspiration for many other churches in the region. The façade, with high windows and much sculpture (note the door of the lions on the north side) is very striking despite its unfinished towers. The interior is suitably grand with fine capitals to the marble columns and mosaic floor. There are several museums including an important archeological collection and the Pinacotèca Provinciale with pictures and works from the 12th century to the 18th. There is a **Motel Agip** outside the city with a good restaurant and **La Pignata** (080-232481) comes highly recommended.

From Bari take the coast road towards Monopoli which occasionally joins with the N16 ribboning its way along the shore but avoiding city centres. Pass through the resorts of S. Giorgio and Torre a Mare to **MOLA DI**

Trulli

BARI with a high-towered castle and many-sided corner bastions. This was a Crusades port, and there was an early church but the present cathedral is 16th century with remnants of the older structure incorporated, including a rose window. Next comes **POLIGNANO A MARE**, with high-walled houses picturesquely perched on the edge of cliff, looking over the sea. Below the village are two caves known as the Grotte Palazzese, which may be visited. Other caves can be visited by boat. There are fine views as you leave the village and head towards **MONOPOLI**, if you wish to continue directly to Fasano, on N16. The main route leaves this sea-eroded coast with its villages and heads inland to Conversano along a country road leading towards the long terraces of the Murge. (This is traversed later in the route.) **CONVERSANO** on its hill is probably the ancient Norba of the Romans and has a Norman castle, much altered over the centuries although the keep is still obvious over the tiled roofs and later towers. There are fine views from here. The duòmo is 14th-century (restored) with much sculptured decoration over its main door and two towers. Nearby is the convent of the Benedictines with elements of Romanesque work and a cloister of the same date with sculpted capitals to its columns. Continue on the route to Castellana Grotte with its famous and highly coloured limestone caves with crystalline formations — well worth a visit. Other caves can be found at **PUTIGNANO** to the south on 377 with rose-coloured alabaster. Note the 14th-century Bali Palace. This side route can take you across to Noci and then Gioia del Colle to join a shortened version of the main route. The route continues towards **FASANO** with its elegant 16th-century palace where you may make a detour to view the ancient site of **Egnazia** towards the sea. This settlement of Greek and Messapian origins has Roman remains and sections of wall, as well as rock-cut tombs. Nearby **SAVELLETRI** on the sea has a pleasant beach.

You are now in the country of the *trulli* and as you proceed towards **OSTUNI** which stands on a rank of hills amidst olive trees, its collection of white buildings clustered around a cathedral with an elaborate façade above alleys climbing steeply upwards within the circle of its walls, you will see examples of these habitations. More will be seen along the route, especially if you make a detour to **ALBEROBELLO** from Martina Franca, which is reached after turning right at **CEGLIE MESSAPICO** with its 15th-century castle. Ceglie was the ancient Caelium. Alberobello, on the road to Noci, has a whole collection of *trulli* — very old dwellings, like beehives with pointed tile roofs — in its Monti quarter. At **MARTINA FRANCA** (pop: 45,000) there are Baroque buildings on its hill over the valley of the Idria; it is a picturesque wine-producing town and you might like to try the local vintage at its restaurants — suggested **Da Antonietta** (080-706511) or a rather more expensive menu at the **Hotel Park San Michele** in a handsome location in the town (080-705520). [A side trip from here can take you either to the already mentioned *trulli* at Albarello, via **LOCOROTONDO** with its unusual houses, with triangular gables — from this town built on a circular plan, you can look over the Murge to see many settlements of *trulli* — or south on 172 to **TARANTO**. Here, on its gulf, is an old city pleasantly combined with modern quarters (pop: 240,000) and a naval dockyard second only to La Spezia. There is a much reconstructed duòmo with a Baroque façade, yet interesting restorations; it is to be found on the island site of the *Citta Vecchia* which is connected by a famous swing bridge from the *Citta Nuova* beside a solidly imposing castle with round towers of Spanish origins. There is a very large and complete collection of antiquities at the Museo Nazionale and an extended visit is suggested. At **Gambero Rosso** (099-407762) as you might expect there is fish on offer in a pleasant restaurant. Not far from Taranto on the road to Francavilla Fontana is **GROTTAGLIE** where the ancient pottery to be seen in Taranto's museum is the inspiration for local potters. This is a wine-producing area and there are many caves and grottoes — in the hillside town is a fine Romanesque façade and door to the church, and a castle.]

The main route may be rejoined from Taranto on 7 towards **MASSAFRA**, which is connected by the narrow 581 crossing the Murge from Martina Franca. Massafra is a town of charm with ravines and odd little grottoes with early Christian frescoes. A deep ravine divides the town and there is a castle incorporating a church which has fine views from its terrace. The Palio della Mezzaluna is held on the third Sunday in September, a folk festival. Continue to **MOTTOLA** where there is a 13th-century cathedral and campanile, and more cave churches in the vicinity. [Incidentally, at nearby Castellaneta, Rudolph Valentino was born.] N100 continues to importantly sited **GIOIA DEL COLLE**, where there is a large, severe castle which can be visited — there is a fine court with a Gothic loggia and a museum of local archaeological items from nearby Monte Sannace. Take 171 towards Santeramo in Colle and on to the town of **ALTAMURA** across the high, flattened Murge. The town has is ancient walls from the 5th century BC still in place, although much reduced and fragmentary. There is a duòmo with a heavily sculptured doorway and a fine rose window, and a striking campanile. The 13th-century walls which gave the

Vase from Taranto National Museum

137

town its name still exist in remnants. The route continues to **GRAVINA IN PUGLIA** although a restaurant of Altamura is worth noting — **U Cecatidde**, a gastronomic landmark (080-841453). At Gravina, a town set in very striking position at the edge of a ravine with several interesting churches — including one, S. Michele, entirely cut out of the rock, is the appropriately-named **La Grotta** which is presided over by a formidable cook-patronne and serves Apulian wines (080-851776). Our route winds across to Ruvo di Puglia but you can take a road direct to Corato and the shore if wished by following 378 about 14km from Gravina.

RUVO DI PUGLIA was famous for its vases and a collecion is on show at Palazzo Jatta. There is a grand late Romanesque duòmo, heavily ornamented and with a splendid campanile. There is a handsome 15th-century courtyard at the Palazzo Spada. Continue on to **CORATO** with its round medieval centre and churches, along the eastern edge of the Murge. Here, or at Ruvo, you may make a diversion to see the curious **Castel del Monte**, famous for its design which is pure Gothic. There are eight octagonal towers and a superb panorama from the top. From Corato the route goes to **ANDRIA** with its 18th-century *Palazzo Ducale* and a cathedral which contains in its crypt the tomb of an English queen, Isabella, the third wife of Frederick II.

We drive on to **CANOSA DI PUGLIA** along N98. On a hill above the Ofanto, this is the old Canusium which has been much excavated. It was renowned for the quality of its figured vases and polychrome works. There is a fine bishop's throne with elephants in the duòmo and the remains of a castle (views) as well as some Roman ruins. Cross the autostrade on 93 towards Barletta and the coast, stopping half-way to view the ruins at **Cannae**. There are extensive excavations of the Roman town and a large necropolis has produced very ancient painted pottery. At **BARLETTA** there is a cathedral with connections to Richard Coeur de Lion and outside the church of S. Sepolcro is the *Colosso*, a giant bronze statue of the 5th century BC. There is also, beside the harbour, a vast castle. Take the coast road for **TRANI**, a wide

Castel del Monte

harbour surrounded with white buildings, where the wines are made from the Muscat (*moscato*) grape, very full and dark red. There is a well-sited cathedral with a restored Romanesque interior and a castle. Next along the coast with its vineyards and olives comes **BISCEGLIE**, with a cathedral in its old section and then **MOLFETTA**, its medieval buildings and cathedral towers reflected in a tranquil harbour, home of a large fishing fleet, and **GIOVINAZZO** with a pleasing ancient centre and a cathedral with Romanesque columns in its crypt. The road passes the airport and so back to Bari.

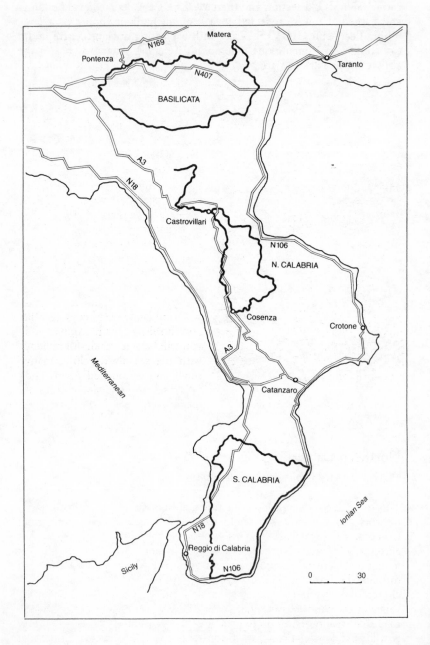

View of bay, Calabrian coast

The deep south of Italy is a dramatic and intriguing region, hardly known to many visitors, and little known to Italians themselves, although it has a band of true aficionados who love this hot and sun-baked land that yet possesses many forests and undiscovered wild lands. Calabria is the long, south-dipping toe of the Italian boot and it is well worth discovering. Also little-known and with interest of its own is the region of Basilicata which is the stretch of valley and hills between Calabria and Apulia. This is a part of Italy many people merely drive through, snaking down the autostrada from Rome and the north towards Reggio di Calabria and the ferry for Sicily. It's a pity not to leave the mercilessly hurrying cars and take a long breath in this ancient and beautiful land. Combine Calabria and Basilicata with Apulia and you will have a wonderful holiday with the sea always close, many small and untouched towns and villages, and just inland a range of scenery that may well surprise you.

Northern Calabria

1 day or longer/235km/start from Latronico

This route does not centre on one town, although there are suggestions as to where to stay and you could easily do it as a circular route from Cosenza or Castrovillari. The assumption is that you will come down the autostrada to Lauria Nord (or else along the more scenic yet winding 19) to exit on the main road running east towards Episcopia. Follow this road through the Basilicata countryside past **LATRONICO** where there is a church of S. Egidio containing a statue of the saint, and go on along the valley of the Sinni towards Episcopia where we turn right down a valley road that rapidly climbs up the valley of the Torrente Frido. The country is wild and lonely. [You can if you wish continue towards Francavilla

141

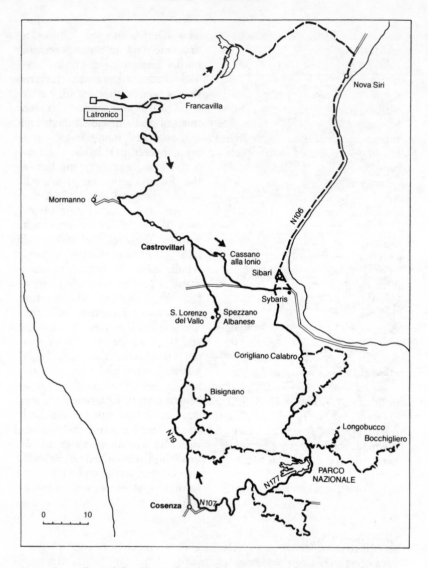

down the valley of the Sinni, for ravishing views, and visits to such towns as Chiaromonte and Senise, but you will need to retrace your route to rejoin this one, for in the mountains the roads are few and often end in cul de sacs. Your one possibility is to go on to the coast at Nova Siri following N106 south along the sea.]

The road meanders through wild scenery around Monte Serra, and to the west can be seen the Lucano range of the Apennines. You cross into Calabria at Coppola di Paola and once over the pass descend towards the autostrada and the road south at the Campotonese exit. A little way west is **MORMANNO**, a village in the upper Lao valley. There is a church with gilded carvings and a 16th-century baptismal font. Our winding road takes us on towards Castrovillari and passes on the right the resort village of **MORANO CALABRO** in the valley of the Coscile, spread on a steep hillside, with narrow streets ascending past several interesting churches — S. Bernardo has been restored to its 15th-century form. There is a ruined castle, originally Norman. The village is a good centre for hiking and walking in the Pollino hills. This vast calcareous *massiccio* which you have just traversed is unique geologically in Calabria, where other mountain ranges are crystalline or sedimentary. It is hoped that the region will become a protected nature park — unusual trees include the Calabrian pine, and there are many wildflowers. Wolves can still be found here, though they are almost as rare as the golden eagles which were once much more numerous. Easter and mid-August (Ferragosto) traditions still survive and you may well be offered local cheese in village eating-places.

Follow the road on towards Castrovillari, although you can make a detour down 105 to the village of **SARACENA** on the edge of the Pollina, set on a jutting spur of land. Here you can try local mountain mushrooms and also the wine of the Pollina — there is a ruined 13th-century castle. **CASTROVILLARI** has an ancient centre, clustered tightly on a rock; the modern town is situated on surrounding flatlands. There is a 15th-century castle with round towers. There is an exceptionally good restaurant here; **Alia** (the family name) is not cheap but it is a wonderful place to find (098-21715). Calabrian food has the reputation of being simple and plain, yet it can be very inventive and it is also healthy, using natural foods.

From here go east to join 19 and then south until a turning to the left indicates **CASSANO ALLO IONIO** with its frescoed duòmo (17th-century belltower), and medieval crypt. Good centre for walks. The road continues down the valley of the Elano until it comes to Doria and the main road east crossing the Piano di Sibari. The alternative road joins here, and you could visit **SIBARI** where there are tourist attractions and watersports and nearby the ancient town of **Sybaris** (which gave its name to the lovers of pleasure, the Sybarites), destroyed by the Crotons, which stood on the banks of the Crathis river. You can visit Sybaris-Thurium (Thurii), a later settlement near the mouth of the present Crati. Continue south across the Plain of Sibari on 106 across several rivers to arrive at **CORIGLIANO CALABRO**. The road offers very good views of the distant mountains of the Sila Greca which can often bear snow on the high points. Corigliano has a large Baroque church and a castle once belonging to the family of the Sansoverino. There is a festival of citrus fruits in January. The road goes on up tight bends into the hills of the Sila, an area of crystalline rocks with extensive woodland and marvellous air. Much of the wood is pine forest, but there is open space too, and lakes. It is excellent for walks, for swimming in the lakes, and for winter sports. [Ascending by the Coz. di Pesco, you can also approach from the town of **ROSSANO**, with its several fine churches and at the Diocesan Museum a rare copy of a 6th-century Greek codex. Not far from the two towns is the *covento del Patire*, approached along a narrow road which goes no farther than this magnificently sited building founded by St Nilus and a once-renowned seat of monastic learning.]

The road continues through the Sila Greca and then the Sila Grande with spectacular scenery as it borders the Parco Nazionale della Calabria. The Sila is not essentially a mountain range, rather a plateau with heights up to 1,928m (Monte Botte) but there are remarkable features — steep river valleys, fast-flowing streams, gorges and lakes. A very large lake abuts the road at the juncture of the park (the Lago di Cecita) but before this on the alternative route from Rossano you pass through the village of **LONGOBUCCO**, a high settlement in the valley of the Trionto, dramatically set. Here women make the textiles that have been produced in Calabria for centuries: rugs and cloths are woven and dyed with naturally produced plant-colourings, and the patterns are traditional and eye-catching, usually of Byzantine influence. This was once a centre for silkworms, exported to Constantinople. Weaving is an ancient art and another centre is at **BOCCHIGLIERO** on the route to the east following 282. The **Parco Nazionale della Calabria** is strikingly scenic, covers 18,000 hectares and was inaugurated in 1968. There are camping sites and many ideal spots for picnics.

[An alternative road shortens the route here, crossing the Sila towards N19, north of the Lago di Cecita and giving good views as it winds along the ridge — 279 crosses the Crati and arrives at the main road just north of Cosenza.] The main route goes on south of the lake and arrives up the valley of a stream at the village of **CAMIGLIATELLO**, at the junction of N107. This is a winter mountain resort, with cable connections, and a festival of mushrooms held in honour of the splendid funghi found here in the early autumn.

Gradually we leave the alpine heights as the road goes on towards Cosenza — but first do make a visit to the little settlement of **FAGO**, where there are springs of mineral waters (excursions possible to Monte Botte Donato and Lake Arvo). The road bends south past Monte Scuro and arrives at **SPEZZANO DELLA SILA**, a well-situated village, with views over towards Cosenza. There is a church with a fine 15th-century door. Next to the village is **CELICO**, the birthplace of the abbot and prophet Gioacchino who founded the Badia Florense at **SAN GIOVANNI IN FIORE** (west on 107), the principal town of the Sila, where women make traditional textiles and often wear particularly fetching local costume.

COSENZA (pop: 110,000) is a provincial capital on the Crati and is suggested as a place to stay for this route (alternative is Castrovillari, directly north on N19). It has an old section on a hillside and a more modern part on flat land — here can be found the University of Calabria, one of the country's most modern institutions of learning. The cathedral, having received the Baroque treatment in the 18th and 19th centuries, has been returned to its original Gothic, French-style elegance. In the museum close by is a fantastic 13th-century reliquary — visible on request to the office, and a tomb of note in the duòmo is that of Isabella of

Aragon, wife of Philippe la Hardi (Duke of Burgundy and King of France), who fell from her horse and died in childbirth here. Winding footways take you up the Via del Seggio past several churches of note and the way to the castle, which was built originally in Norman times and was the scene of the marriage of Margaret of Savoy. It is now ruined, but its polygonal keep is impressive, dating from 1222. Excellent views over the old town with its tall, roof-tiled houses and the two rivers, the Crati and the Busento. A recommended restaurant is **La Calavrisella** with local and Calabrese dishes at reasonable prices (0984-28012).

The route goes on from Cosenza north to Castovillari — as already stated you may choose the N19 or go fast on the E1 autostrada. N19 follows the valley of the Crati most of the way. At Bivio Rose it is joined by 279 (alternative route from the national park). Just before this a road branches left to **MONTALTO UFFUGO**, a summer resort with fine woodcarvings in its churches. Chestnuts (fresh and dried) and mushrooms can be bought here. Farther along N19 at Bivio Acri a road goes right towards the high village of **LUZZI** — which may be the ancient Lucanian Thebes. Women wear traditional costume and make special cakes, the *piattatissime*, for an August festival at Sambucina Abbey. You can continue on this detour towards the little town of **BISIGNANO** with its duòmo with wooden sculptures and the cloisters of the Riforma church. Locally made are lutes (and other string instruments, including violins) and there are potteries in the area, too. Rejoin the route on N19 and continue north via Tarsia to **SPEZZANO ALBANESE** where there are spa baths of various waters from chalybeate, chlorine, iodine, alkaline and bromide springs. The tall inhabitants of this hillside town show they are of Albanian origin. Across the main road from Spezzano is **S. LORENZO DEL VALLO** in the Esaro valley with a restored castle above the village: interesting paintings in the church.

The road continues with a possible detour on 534 to the left taking you to **LUNGRO** via Firmo. Here local wines may be tried and other specialities are the pecorino cheeses and mutton dishes. The main church, containing a fine madonna painted on wood, follows the Greek rite. Return to N19 (or take the very winding 105) back to Castrovillari and the end of the route.

Southern Calabria
1 or 2 days/285km/from Vibo

Although this route is based on Vibo in the north, other centres could equally well be chosen: perhaps Rosarno, or Palmi, or Reggio di Calabria in the west, or any of the numerous small seashore resorts along the Ionian Sea.

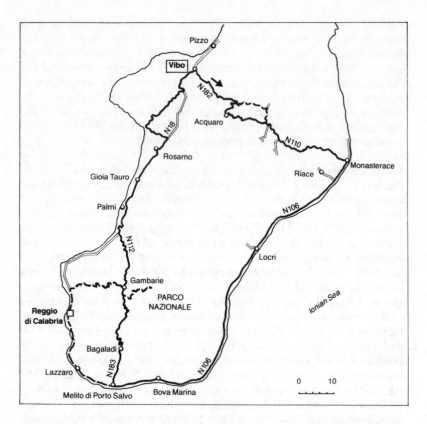

VIBO (Vibo Valentia to give its full name, pop: 32,000) is a town standing in a fine position above the Gulf of Sant'Eufemia. There is a castle, Norman in origin, with an archaeological collection, and some narrow medieval streets have been replaced (due to earthquakes) with wider thoroughfares. The town was an important centre in the late 18th century when it was a provincial capital under French domination (the King of Naples later lost his life when he attempted to return in 1815). There is a port and a resort at Vibo Marina. The town itself is a modern, lower section, but in the old town visit the many churches (most with some damage due to earthquake) and the Palazzo Gagliardi which has items from Hipponium, a Greek settlement which once occupied the site of Vibo. There are ruins of a Roman bath at Sant'Aloe. Greek remains include a Doric temple and the fragments of the town walls with the bases of towers. August events include a festival of local crafts and religious arts, as well as cinema events. A good place to stay is the **Hotel 501**, which also boasts a restaurant of note with a terrace (0963-43951).

The route begins below the town on 182 heading east, first towards Piscopio. Cross the autostrada A3 past S. Angelo and continue to **SORIANO CALABRO**, where you will find a village on a slope with the ruined church of San Domenico, destroyed by earthquake yet preserving a good Baroque façade. The church of the Carmine has a splendid wooden choir — the town is still a good centre for handicrafts, and local people make items in cane and wickerwork. On sale are local wine and honey. The neighbouring village of **SORIANELLO** has a ruined medieval castle and, in the church, a wooden crucifix of the 16th century attributed to a Flemish artist, David Muller. One road leaves the village and climbs up through woods to **SERRA S. BRUNO** with a wood-working population, living in pretty decorated houses, as a suggested detour. The main route zig-zags south towards Acquaro, but turn left before this village is reached to go to **ARENA**. Here on a hill there are ruins of a Norman castle and the church has 18th-century statues in wood. Drive on through woods (the bosco di S. Maria) up to and over the Colle d'Arena at 1099m. The 110 now descends the river valleys along a very twisting road to the Ionian coast below. At Monte Pecoraro a road to the right takes you to **FABRIZIA**, a well-placed resort on the Ionian side of the Serre range where there are good walks. Good mushrooms from the woods; local weaving. The road should be regained by going back and then looking for a picnic site if it is lunchtime — this is idyllic countryside for an *al fresco* meal of local cheese and wine!

The views on this side of the Serre are truly magnificent, with sea views on a clear day. The mountains are impressive, the scenery wooded and wild, often rock-strewn. To the right is a turning for **NARDODIPACE** and its older village; the former is a new settlement replacing one farther down the valley that was flooded. 110 goes on through many curves until it arrives at **PAZZANO** beside Monte Stella in the Silaro valley, where there is a grotto-sanctuary (frescoes) and a huge 16th-century sculpture. Ahead is Monte Consolino and just to the left of the route is **STILO**, above a river flowing through a gorge, a village set against the rocky slopes of the mountain and with a jewel at its heart — the Cattolica. This is a church of Byzantine origin, and is built on a traditional square plan with small conical drums — it was originally thought to date to the 6th or 7th century, but is now believed to be 10th century. It has interesting brick decoration on the outside, and within four antique marble columns reversed, and damaged frescoes — yet it is still considered one of the best preserved Byzantine buildings in existence. There are other churches in this dramatically placed mountain village, notable ruined San Domenico and the 16th-century San Francesco. The area has many grottoes, some with frescoes. The road continues down the Stilaro valley to arrive at Monasterace Marina on the coast, where the route turns right, although a visit might be made just to the north to see the ruins of Greek **Caulonia** where there are temple walls excavated earlier this century. Up from the shore here **MONASTERACE** on a hill has 16th-century fortifications and a ruined castle.

The road runs south (106) to **RIACE MARINA** where in 1972 a pair of bronze warriors were found in the sea. Behind the beach resort is the medieval town of **RIACE** with walls and gates. The road continues along the beautiful Ionian shore, its spacious beaches (rarely crowded, and sandy) backed by mountains. A stop is suggested at **LOCRI**, on the seashore and with a museum (collezione Scaglione) devoted to finds from **Locri Epizefri**, about 4km from the modern town. Here, over a large area, you can visit excavated walls, temples and military constructions and a well-marked theatre. Little remains, but the temples in particular are evocative, and there are unusual ones such as the underground sanctuary of Pan and the Nymphs. Most of the finds are in the Reggio Museum — as are the Riace warriors. From here there are a series of beaches all the way to the southernmost cape, but back in the hills can be found fascinating places — a side trip from Locri takes you up to **GERACE**, a medieval town with a ruined castle and extensive defensive systems, as well as a fine 11th-century cathedral with an apse in Byzantine style. The coast road goes on to round the promontory, passing through small seaside places backed by citrus orchards and vineyards (there is much local wine here) and with interesting crafts on sale — linen, woodcarving, pottery. The route curves west at **CAPO SPARTIVENTO**, the ancient Heracleum Promontorium with a wide beach facing the translucent sea. This is the Costa dei Gelsomini, backed by hills. **BOVA MARINA** is one of the towns of Greek origin (five in all) and here can be found Roman ruins. There is a small harbour at the mouth of the Sideroni and fishing and water sports. 106 goes on until the route leaves it at Melito de Porto Salvo where we drive inland.

[An alternative is to continue on to **REGGIO DI CALABRIA** (pop: 174,000) on the coast road, and to rejoin the main route by a mountainous road going right from Gallico on 184 into the Aspromonte to S. Stefano. Reggio is a port for Sicily on the Straits of Messina, a mostly modern city due to earthquakes, but there is a well-preserved towered castle of the 15th century. The National Museum has a prehistoric collection and many works brought together from Magna Grecia. The city is also a resort, and in its restaurant local specialities can be found. Recommended are **Bonaccorso** (0965-96048) with fish featured, and the restaurant at the **Hotel Miramare** (0965-91881), with its terrace and fine view as far as Sicily's Etna on a good day. Both of these are reasonable in price.]

A street scene in Calabria

Our route turns onto 183 up into the wild heights of the massif of Aspromonte. This vast mountain has a sugar loaf appearance — with sheer drops to the west and rugged slopes to the east. It is heavily wooded and has ski-slopes on its heights at Gambarie. The scenery is wild and desolate, the terrain arid and rugged, dotted with the ubiquitous olive trees (olive oil is sold in most shops and is very good; olives also feature in local cooking). The road climbs up this last outcrop of the Apennines to arrive at Bagaladi, then takes a series of steep curves to cross the mountainside with views up to the range (highest is Mte Montalto, also highest point of Calabria). 183 continues past the National Park beyond Croce di Romeo, or farther along, on the right, for a detour to this high nature preserve. Some of the Aspromonte has been turned to agriculture since the cutting of the original forests, but a re-afforestation programme is in operation. We leave Mte Basilica to the right and come into the **GAMBARIE** ski region at S. Stefano in Aspromonte where the detour to Reggio rejoins the route. This thickly wooded area has many walks and excursions, and the Gambarie winter-sports resort offers a chair lift to the Puntone di Scirocco at 1,660m and regular ski-lifts.

The descent towards the charmingly named *Costa Viola* (Violet coast — supposedly because of the sunsets) begins shortly, across the *Piani di Aspromonte* and we leave the 183 to continue inland as the route follows 112 down a wriggling road towards the sea. The road crosses the autostrada A3 and arrives at Pellegrina, to turn right. [A detour may be made to the left, however, to visit **SCILLA**, a ravishingly pretty fishing village on a rocky promontory at the northern end of the Straits of Messina. There is a castle and local specialities include swordfish, which may be fished for here and eaten accompanied with local wines in several varieties, notably the delicious cherry-coloured *cerasuola*.]

The road zig-zags above the coast which is threaded with a railway line, and after about 14km N8 arrives at **PALMI**, just off the road on the shore, overlooking the Tyrrhenian Sea. It is a modern town, several times decimated by earthquakes, but now rebuilt according to anti-seismic knowledge. It has a good public garden, several museums and a library. On the last Sunday of August there is a major religious procession. A detour may be made to climb Monte Sant'Elia for the fine views.

The route passes through **GIOIA TAURO**, after enjoying impressive views across the straits. The old town stands on a cliff, and there is a beach. It is noted as the site of **Metaurum**, with a Greek necropolis. We go inland to arrive at **ROSARNO** with its Baroque clocktower. Walks can be made to ancient **MEDMA** and its necropolis. To the left is the vast area of the **Capo Vaticano** with superb shorelines of dramatic beauty. These can be sampled instead of returning directly to Vibo on N18. [A detour from the starting point is suggested to **PIZZO** on the Gulf of Sant'Eufemia, a charming village on a cliff with a castle and local crafts (basketwork) and a festival of the sea in July. A local restaurant is **Medusa**, a fish place open most of the time (0963-231203).]

Basilicata
1-2days/340km/from Matera

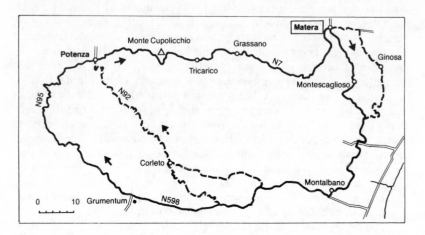

This is one of the wildest and poorest regions of Italy, and the driving or walking is not easy since Basilicata is mostly mountain and sharp-sided valleys. For those with a curiosity about the less-known Italy, it makes a fascinating study, however, and in the forests rare wild animals still exist. There are two possibilities as bases, Potenza, which is closer to communications, and Matera, which is the more interesting and attractive town.

MATERA (pop: 50,000) is well situated beside a ravine and in the rock caves (the *sassi*) people still live among chapels hollowed from the rock. (There are many such places around Matera, some with fine frescoes.) In the town is the 13th-century duòmo, with a campanile, and the interior, while redesigned in the 18th century, has not been completely destroyed — there are intricate capitals upon the antique columns. There is a Renaissance chapel and a remarkable 16th-century crib, hollowed from the rock, with many figures. There are other interesting churches, a museum with pieces from surrounding excavations (the Museo Ridola, closed Mon) and superb views from many streets. Processional ceremony 2 July, with a tournament. Good, inexpensive restaurants — try **Sorangelo** (0835-216719) for good meats.

Drive from Matera down the side of the valley on 175 to arrive at the handsome village of **MONTESCAGLIOSO**, with a big church amidst whitewashed houses and an abbey. Continue on to cross the Bradano below, then turn left on 380 to **BERNALDA** where there is a castle. [A detour from Matera could also have taken in **GINOSA** with its 11th-century castle and in the neighbouring Gravina, troglodyte houses — its marina has a beach.] A jog to the right on N407 takes you over the

Basento, then turn right to cross a number of valleys to Montalbanico Ionico. Leave this backroad to turn right on N598 along the valley of the Agri. The road continues through wild scenery along the river until it arrives at the Lago di Pietra del Pertusillo and the ancient site of **GRUMENTUM** just south of the lake. (An alternative route for the adventurous could take you up various mountain roads via **CORLETA** with its castle, through woods where boar and wolf still live, to make a cut across to Potenza.) Our route gives views of this terrain on a good road, with parallel roads a possibility for exploration. It goes on to pass Paterno as the Agri dwindles in its valley and we continue on to

Red peppers drying in the sun

BRIENZA with its castle. A winding mountain road takes us across valleys to **SATRIANO**, an ancient site beyond the village of the same name, and then leaves 95 to turn right and parallel the autostrada into Potenza.

POTENZA (pop: 60,000), a town of modern aspect, stands at a considerable height (820m) and has been badly affected by both quake and warfare; there is little of atmosphere or architectural interest left to see. Its ancient cathedral has been rebuilt, although it retains an original rose window. It stands in a commanding position, but other churches are of more interest, notably S. Michele (restored Romanesque), near the theatre, S. Francesco with 15th-century doorways and campanile and S. Maria del Sepulcro (restored 13th century). The Museo Archeologico contains many local 'finds' from the excavations at **Metaponto** and other sites in the Lucano (closed Mon). There is a festival in May. In Potenza try **Mimi** for local dishes (0971-28673).

Take the main road east, 7, until you arrive at Brindisi Montagna where you turn left to climb up above the valley of the Basento which cuts a valley down from Potenza. [Earlier note **VAGLIO BASILICATA**, a town of medieval origin with a church of the Baroque containing carved and gilded wood, or another expedition can be made to **ACERENZA**, farther off, and also on a hilltop, to see the fine 13th-century duòmo with its odd round tower and fine west door.] The route is well wooded and wild, as you turn right and skirt the slopes of Monte Cupolicchio, up the pass of Valico until on the other side you come to **TRICARICO**, with its fortress, a round-towered Norman construction. There are several churches in this medieval hill-town, and in the surroundings relics of Roman occupation as well as earlier tombs. The route goes on with fine views from the ridge, until **GRASSANO** to the left with frescoes in a convent, now the *Municipio*. At **MIGLIONICO** the castle stands out above the deeply cut gorge of the Bradano; there are churches with interesting details, one with a Romanesque campanile, another with a Cima Madonna and Child. Here you can make a diversion down the main road, N7, or take backroads, to **FERRANDINA** where there is a good restaurant, *Degli Ulivi* (0835-757020), in a town taken over by industry (underground resources of methane gas) — the restaurant is charming, however.

The road goes north from Miglionico to cross the Bradano passing **Lake San Giuliano** (artificial but pretty) and on up through ravines to arrive back at Matera.

13 THE ISLANDS

Even a cursory glance at a map will show that there are many islands around the long, sea-surrounded Italian peninsula, dipping its toe far towards the south and the coast of Africa. From the marshy islets of the Venetian Lagoon to the volcanic upthrustings of the Lipari islands you could spend many holidays and still not see them all. The islands most worth exploring are the big, roughly triangular, Sicily (Italian: Sicilia) and the almost rectangular Sardinia (Sardegna). The capital of Sicily, Palermo, is only a little farther from Tunis than it is from Reggio di Calabria, the main departure point from the Italian mainland. It follows that this island should be almost African in some of its aspects. Hot, dusty and surprisingly varied, it has many surprises and exotic aspects, as well as some disagreeable qualities most marked in the west where towns are often badly looked after and that ancient Sicilian establishment, the Mafia, is most deeply rooted. You will find marvels everywhere however, from the fish restaurants to the gleaming beaches, from the mysterious Greek ruins to the great cathedral at Monreale. The island has an essence and a character not easily found, yet one that exerts a powerful charm for many visitors.

Sardinia is quite different, a place of green mountains, rocks and a secret interior with marvellous views over the Mediterranean. It depends south of the small French island of Corsica, and has many similar qualities. It is farther from the mainland than Sicily, and this makes it more remote, more atmospheric and very much its own place. You can't hurry here — the roads are often rough and winding, but the scenery is splendid so you won't want to. Probably the best way to enjoy Sardinia is from a small self-catering place, though there are good small hotels especially in coastal resort areas. Both islands have their own character, and both repay a long and detailed exploration — a week or two will pass quickly, and you will discover that while both islands are Italian they have much of their own essence to offer, too.

Sardinia
1 or 2 days/420km/from Cagliari

This trip really does need more than a day although by cutting some of

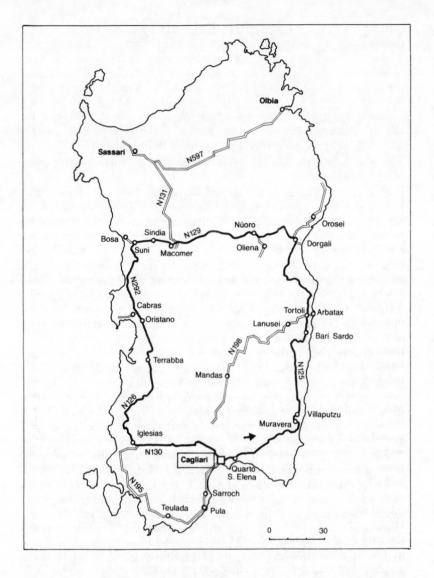

the smaller side roads and using the main 131 and 131d you could do it; or cut it in two separate halves. Base yourself at **CAGLIARI** (pop: 200,000) at one of several hotels or guest houses, and explore the island's capital. It is a city with big panoramas and you can start by going up to the Umberto I Terrace for the view over the city and over the lagoons around the harbour. Above is the cathedral, with a Baroque interior but some remnants of its Gothic origins. There is a museum in the cathedral and also a *Museo Archeologico* on the Piazza Indipendenza, next to the 14th-century tower of S. Pancrazio with the ancient town walls beyond. The museum contains objects from the island's past and a floor of pictures, as well as folklore collections. A walk along the ramparts of the fortifications (Pisan 14th century) brings a view of the Elephant Tower. The wide Largo Carlo Felice with its trees has good shops and leads you to the Piazza Matteotti, with the 19th-century town hall at the heart of the town. From here the Via Roma goes along the port, with arcaded buildings stretching to the Maritime Station. There is a Roman amphitheatre and a Botanic Garden: the theatre is carved from the hillside. Places to eat in Cagliari include the expensive **Dal Corsaro** (070-664318) in the centre or less expensive **Buongustaio** (070-668124). The **Motel Agip** at the approaches to the town is also recommended (070-561645).

Leave Cagliari on the road towards the east, N125, passing near to **QUARTO S. ELENA**, where white wine is produced and a folk festival is held each May. The plain, fertile and green, begins to change to hills and rocky scenery and the road climbs through mountains passing at one point *nuraghe* — ancient stone towers of conical shape that at one time served as fortified places of safety. At **S. PRIAMO** you can look over the sea and here the road turns left towards **MURAVERA** and **VILLAPUTZU**, two villages surrounded with orchards of almond, orange and lemon trees. The road from here is very scenic, going north amidst mountains that are often unusually coloured. At **BARI SARDO** there are more *nuraghe* close by. The road goes on to **TORTOLI** and its nearby seaside branch of **ARBATAX** with a lighthouse and picturesque red-rocked resort with nice views. [From Tortoli, on the edge of its plain, you can take a short cut back to Cagliari if wished via Lanusei and **MANDAS** on 198 and 128. At Mandas there are old wooden statues in the church and prehistoric constructions not far off.] From Tortoli N125 goes through a surprisingly scenic region — the *stagno di Tortoli* is passed and pink rocks mound up with sudden views until you arrive at **BANEI** where there is a Baroque church with a belltower on the mountainside and a terrace for viewing the valley below. Onwards the scenery becomes more impressive, if severe, with more wide-ranging views, as you proceed inland a bit. The road then goes down along a charming descent into the village of Dorgali. Before you arrive you may like to turn right and visit the bathing spot known as **Cala Gonone** which has several good grottoes in the neighbourhood. The route turns inland towards Nuoro along a valley, but an interesting detour can be made up to **OROSEI**, beside the sea with a charming situation and the ruins of a castle as well as several churches. The route passes, just beyond Dorgali, the group of constructions known as the *nuraghe Serra Orrios*; about 70 of them can be seen.

NUORO (pop: 27,000), an important town, stands below Mte Ortobene. It is a popular resort with many excursions possible into the surrounding countryside and up into the mountains. There are prehistoric tombs and folk costumes can be seen — the village of **S. OLIENA** to the south-east has a fine situation and good local wines. The top of the mountain is marred with a statue, but the terrace offers good views. A

Sardinian brooch

good restaurant in Nuoro is **Del Grillo** (0784-32005) reasonable with local cooking. There is a Baroque church and on the S. Onofrio hill a costume museum, while the Nuoro cathedral terrace offers a good panorama.

Continue on towards Macomer, crossing the main 131 and following the backroad with its good views. **MACOMER** is an important junction beneath the mountains, and cheese is made locally. *Nuraghe* are also found close by and merit a visit. The **Motel Agip** (0785-71066) offers a good and low-priced meal here.

Follow the 129 bis out of town towards Suni. [You can instead, if you wish to explore the northern part of the island, follow the main 131 to **SASSARI** from Macomer, however, and the island's second largest town still preserves a large part of its medieval centre with the duòmo at its heart. It is an odd Spanish-influenced church with highly detailed decorations on the front of the building with a portico. S. Maria di Betlem is more imposing, with a fine early doorway. May is a big month in Sassari with festivals of folk costume and an artisans' fair, while in August the town goes Spanish in a festival on 15 August with enormous gilded candles. From Sassari you can make many expeditions into the mountains and as far as **OLBIA** on the Costa Smeralda — a port on the gulf with connections to the mainland by ferry boat. **Pozzo Sacro** (0789-21033) is a good restaurant in comfortable rustic style and plain, good food at reasonable cost.]

The route passes through **SINDIA** where there is an ancient church of the 12th century and the remains of an abbey of the same date. Beyond Suni you can branch off to **BOSA** if wished to see the ruined castle, and close to the town a good beach and harbour. At Suni you turned left on 292 to pass through **CUGLIARI** with its double-belfried church. Then take the direction of Oristano, passing through forested slopes and olive groves, all very lush against the sea which is reached at **S. CATERINA DI PITTINURI** after the tower. In the neighbourhood is the ruined city of **Cornus** and although little can be seen it is worth a stop. The road crosses a peninsula through lakes (one *stagno* has good fishing) at Cabras, just to the right of the route, and comes to **ORISTANO**, which has some interesting buildings including a Baroque cathedral with a fine early campanile (14th century) and a museum with items from the local excavations at **Tharros**, a Carthaginian city of antiquity with ruins of temples. The site, beyond Cabras, can be visited.

Follow the signs for N131 south towards Cagliari but branch off to the right at the sign for **TERRALBA**. (Just before, at S. Giusta, is a good

12th-century church.) The road goes south to **GUSPINI** with a Gothic church. The town is the centre for expeditions into the mountains and the zinc mines found there. Soon the road rises into the hills and passes through Fluminimaggiore where there are mines, and continues through fine scenery to **IGLESIAS** (pop: 19,000). This town has a school of mines and is a centre for the industry. There is a castle and parts of the old city wall, as well as the preserved façade of the cathedral (inside is much later) from 1290. From Iglesias a direct road, 130, strikes directly east to Cagliari. If you wish you could stop at the *Grotta di S. Giovanni* to see the stalactites and other formations in a long cave. An alternative is to take the longer coast road by way of **TEULADA**, a pretty village situated just beyond the mining areas. The drive is by the sea and through evergreen woods. At **PULA** you may visit the ruins of **Nora** an ancient Phoenician city, later Roman. As you arrive at **SARROCH** you will have fine views, and a little farther on the skyline of Cagliari can be seen.

Sicily

1, 2 or more days/480km/from Taormina

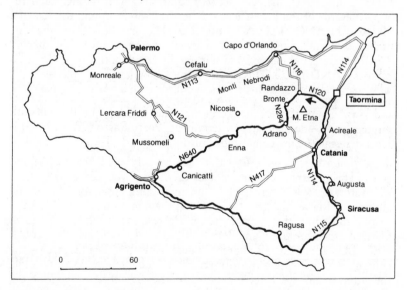

This is a very large island, and you should not attempt too much in the often-enervating heat and dust of country roads. This route, although presented as one, is, like the previous one to Sardinia, intended as a guide and to be broken up into small sections for slow perambulations to appreciate better these intriguing places.

The route is planned around **TAORMINA** (pop: 15,000) but can easily be broken at such cities as Siracusa, Palermo, Cefalu or Agrigento.

Taormina is an international resort of considerable charm on the island's east coast — the three coasts roughly correspond to the three geographical areas of Sicily, the north mountainous, the south and centre hills and plateaus, and the east volcanic. It makes a good spot to stay, being well equipped with hotels and restaurants and a railway station connecting to Messina and the main ferry point from the mainland. In spring and summer it is delightful, its buildings seeming to tumble down a steep hill to the sea, and the town offers many pleasing vistas and spectacles. There is a castle, an impressively sited Greek theatre, the ruined **Naumachia** (Roman) and the 13th-century restored cathedral. Other buildings of Gothic and Renaissance origin can be seen in the town. Restaurants tend to be expensive (this is a smart resort) but try **Giova Rosy Senior** (0942-24411) with its small terrace in the proximity of the *teatro antico*; while you will pay a good deal more at the Hotel Villa S. Andrea's **Oliviero** (0942-23125), you ought to eat very well.

Take the road south towards Catania, running along the shore of the Ionian Sea. The 114 parallels the autostrada which we cross with 185 (or if you miss it, 120) to the right to visit Etna, heading towards Randazzo. **Etna**, often snow-cloaked, is the highest point of the island and still an active volcano. You can ascend to the top and walk through the cindery fields to the craters, the eerie scenery contrasting with the rich orchards and vineyards of the lowest levels. The road winds around through the village of **FRANCAVILLA DI SICILIA**, built in a hollow and the start of a road to Etna's summit which is a well-advised detour full of interest. The route turns right at 185 and starting the circuit of the mountain mass reaches **RANDAZZO**. This medieval town is built of dark volcanic rock, with a severe-looking cathedral and a church with a fine campanile — S. Martino. The town is on the flanks of Etna: opposite are the Monti Nebrodi which can be traversed up the road leading to **CAPO D'ORLANDO** which is a resort with a castle standing on a prominent point of the north shore. You will climb steeply to the pass before descending to Capo on 116, with wide views, Etna's large mass behind you. [This alternative route could then take you along the shore westwards towards Palermo along an interesting coast road below the autostrada. Many small beach resorts and the interesting site of **TUSA**, a small resort where the ruins of ancient **Halaesa** can be visited — a town founded around 490BC, and developed under the Romans. Next comes **CEFALÙ** with its famous church situated beneath a gigantic rock — the church is Norman and is twin-towered with an impressive doorway, while the interior has spectacular mosaics in the Byzantine manner. From Cefalu it is an easy drive on to Palermo, or you may rejoin the route at Enna, by taking the autostrada from just west of Cefalu — A19.]

Leave Randazzo on 284 continuing Etna's circuit via **BRONTE**, a small high-set village on this road with its superb views. There is a steep descent to **ADRANO**, with its remnants of ancient Greek **Adranon** and a Norman castle. The town sits on the softly sloping south-western flank of Etna, surrounded by vegetation.

[If you wish to make only the Etna circuit, leave the route here and go towards Catania, by way of the busy town of **PATERNO** where the foliage becomes more lush as you follow the Simeto valley. There are good views from the impressive 11th-century castle. At **CATANIA** you find a city that has been much-ravaged by Etna's eruptions and exists now in an 18th-century town-plan configuration. It is Sicily's second city (pop: 350,000) but is dusty and somewhat unkempt. There is a long sea-front and port and a restored castle — now a museum — and impressive Baroque buildings, especially around the cathedral where Catania's famous son, the composer Bellini, is buried. A short drive along the coast road north (114) will take you back to Taormina by way of **ACIREALE** on the sea with a beach and thermal establishments, and several Baroque churches. Acireale faces the sea from its ledge among vineyards, and the islands are those of Faraglioni, the home of the monstrous Cyclops. There are good places to eat in Acireale: note **Barbarossa** (095-604933) where you will find fine fish.]

For the longer tour of the island leave Adrano on 121 east towards Enna. The scenery is hilly and uneven, often surprising, and there are interesting small towns such as **CENTURIPE** with a terrace and good views, and an archaeological museum. Pass through Regalbuto to **AGIRA**, a town with ancient origins — the Greek **Agyrion** — and an attractive castle and Gothic church (S. Salvatore). Continue on through **LEONFORTE** with its fountain, to **ENNA**, handsomely sited on a romantic plateau, the centre of Sicily and known as its 'belvedere'. There are indeed fine views from the town, and more of the Baroque for which Sicily is famous. The cathedral (adapted early from a 14th-century church) has a good Baroque façade. The large castle once sported a score of towers: now there are far fewer but you can climb one for the view; a similar wide-ranging one is offered from the octagonal Torre Federico II. In Enna try the **Centrale** (0935-21025) for low-priced local dishes.

[From Enna you can take another possible alternative route on to **PALERMO**, pop: 600,000, and capital of the island. It is reached from Enna directly on the wriggling 121 by way of Lercara Friddi, where you follow signs via **MISILMERI**, a town of Arabic origins with the remnants of a castle. Palermo has much to offer, but it is a somewhat depressing town, with a rundown ring of suburbs. More spectacular is the Norman palace with its beautiful Palatine Chapel with mosaics and a lush blending of Arab and Norman modes. The five tiny red cupolas of S. Giovanna degli Eremiti give it a toy-like appearance, but it is one of the monuments of Norman art with its cloister in a garden. The vast cathedral is of neo-classical design. There are several other fascinating churches, several museums and an archaeological collection with pieces from the Greek settlements. There is an opera house, which sadly seems almost never to be used. Along the sea-front are several good places to eat, but the best are probably in the town centre. Try **Gourmand's** (091-323431) a moderately expensive place or **La Scudaria** (091-520323). In the locality of Palermo, and easily reached, are the Cuba (a 12th-century building), the Villa Tasca (large garden) and the bizarre catacombs of the Capuchin monastery where you will find a large number of mummified

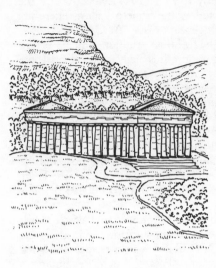

Sicily — Greek ruin

bodies that have dried in the air, or are preserved. This is a remarkable and very Sicilian experience; some corpses are ranged around tables or are seen as they might have been in life. A place that should not be missed on any account is the spectacular cathedral of **Monreale**, just outside Palermo's suburbs. This great Norman church has many marvels (notable mosaics and sculpture) and has a remarkable Arab flavour in its construction. The cloisters are magnificent with over a hundred pairs of elegant columns.]

The main route from Enna goes south-west towards Agrigento on 640. The first principal town is **CALTANISSETTA**, a mining town yet with good buildings (Baroque) and a fine Fountain of Neptune. There are castle ruins on a rocky height, and the town is noted for its procession which takes place on Holy Thursday. Handsome public gardens.

Continue through **CANICATTI**, a mining centre on a hill, to pass **FAVARA** and **NARO**, both towns worth a stop and exploration, particularly the latter — a small settlement on a hill with a good church, castle and remnants of ancient walls. The road arrives at **AGRIGENTO** with fabulous Greek ruins of the city of **Akragas**. The city itself has a medieval centre and a museum of archaeological finds, but after a brief foray you will want to see the temples and tombs of the ancient quarter. They stand along a ridge for the most part and are among the best-preserved remains of the ancient world — the Doric Temple of Concord, the very beautiful contemporary Temple of Juno Lacinia, the Temple of Castor and Pollux and the ruins of the huge Temple of Jupiter are but a few of the stars of Agrigento. Pollution and the pressure of the town are making problems, yet it remains one of the most fascinating remains of antiquity. If you have time, plan to visit the lonely ruins of **Selinunte**, near to Trapini in the east of the island, and equally impressive.

From Agrigento take the coast road towards **GELA**, which also has Greek remains (fortifications) and a museum of finds from local excavations. The town, on a hill, has a port and good views. Before you will have passed through **PALME DI MONTECHIARO**, which was described in *The Leopard*, and **LICATA**, an industrial town. After Gela the road cuts inland towards Vittoria and then **COMISO**, which has ancient remains of a set of Roman baths and a castle: not far off are the ruins of **Camarina**, a Greek settlement. **RAGUSA** merits a stop — it has a Baroque section and is handsomely sited on a ridge. A recommended restaurant here is reasonable **Villa Fortugno** (0932-28656) with local food, some with Arabic origins. Drive on to **MODICA**, which has some interesting churches, and so on along 115 to **NOTO** with its attractive plan of squares and linked streets with vistas. (Before Noto look for signs for the troglodyte dwellings of Ispica.) Pass on through **AVOLA** with groves of almonds — lovely in spring — and so to **SIRACUSA**. This is an ancient town of great importance in the antique world, and although the suburbs are dreary the island of Ortygia is filled with interest — it is the home of the old town (linked by bridge to the sprawl of the city) and its cathedral is fashioned around a Doric temple whose columns are imbedded in the walls. There are many interesting buildings and a very good archaeological museum. On the other side of the town are the ruins of the ancient settlement with a Greek theatre and a Roman amphitheatre, set in gardens that were once quarries. **Jonico** (0931-65540) is a noted restaurant. From Siracusa take 114 north past the oil port of Augusta and a spoiled coast, to arrive at Catania and the already-described route back to Taormina.

BOOKS

Italy produces many publications alluringly laying out the charm of the country, and often the pictures are very enticing. In addition, Italy has been so popular with writers for so long that there are numerous works of travel and fiction that make invaluable background material.

Guidebooks

My tattered old **Hachette World Guide** has been an invaluable companion on many trips, but it does tend to give a French viewpoint even though in English. **The Blue Guides** (A. & C. Black, London; W.W. Norton, New York) are useful and frequently updated. They include detailed city maps, and are written by enthusiastic, knowledgeable people. The little paperback **Welcome to Italy** (Collins) is useful as a reference to quick facts and population totals. Little guidebooks to individual cities are published by Berlitz in a series, and these pocket booklets, illustrated quite well, come with audio tapes in a pack — though credit is not given to an author, merely to 'the staff', and that is not a good sign: I like to know who is telling me what to see and do, and Alta Macadama, for example, infuses certain **Blue Guides** with a large pinch of personality which is attractive.

   Travellers' Handbook, put out by the Italian Tourist Office, is packed with basic useful information. For good food pick up a copy of **La Guida d'Italia** for the current year (Le Guide de l'Espresso, Milan). It *is* in Italian, which is unfortunate if your knowledge is limited, but the signs and indications (points are awarded annually for establishments) are clear. It will also help improve your Italian when you are hungrily checking to see if there is a good restaurant near your base or stopover!

General Interest

Recent books of general interest which I have found illustrative include **Italian Labyrinth** (*John Haycraft*, Penguin) and **Travellers' Italy** (*Arthur Eperon*, Pan).

History and Literature

A history of Italy that is serviceable is **A Concise History of Italy** (American Heritage at Cassell, London). For insights into Italian life, read the novels of *Moravia* (**The Indifferents**), *Malaparte* (**The Tuscans**), *Pratolini* (**The Quarter**), *Carlo Levi* (**Christ Stayed at Eboli**) or *Tomaso di Lampedusa* (**The Leopard**, set in Sicily). *D.H. Lawrence* describes his visit to Etruria in 1927 in **Etruscan Places** (Olive Press, London & Berkeley). Some of these may of course be out of print, and I can only suggest a long browse in second-hand book stores. You may find treasures both beautiful and useful — **Roman Mornings** by James Lee-Milne and **The Italian Lakes** (A. & C. Black, 1905!) came to me this way. Books on Italy, like touring the country itself, are often a question of luck or simple serendipity!

INDEX